BEAUTIFUL AMBIGUITIES

BEAUTIFUL AMBIGUITIES

An Inside View of the Heart of Government

Peter Le Cheminant

Illustrations by Sandy Rogers

The Radcliffe Press
London · New York

Published in 2001 by The Radcliffe Press
6 Salem Road, London W2 4BU
175 Fifth Avenue, New York NY 10010

In the United States and Canada
distributed by St Martin's Press
175 Fifth Avenue, New York NY 10010

ISBN 1–86064–719–7

A full CIP record for this book is available from the British Library
A full CIP record for this book is available from the Library of Congress

Library of Congress Catalog card: available

Typeset in Sabon by Oxford Publishing Services, Oxford
Printed and bound in Great Britain by MPG Books Ltd, Bodmin

Contents

List of Illustrations   *vii*
Acronyms and Abbreviations   *ix*
Introduction   *xiii*

1.   Falling In   1
2.   The World of Work   4
3.   New Colleagues   9
4.   Early Lessons   12
5.   The Posh End of the Business   17
6.   The Dirty End of the Business   22
7.   First Link with the Internet   33
8.   Closer to the Centre   37
9.   Lies, Damn Lies and Statistics   49
10. A Rude Interruption   51
11. Again the Numbers Game   55
12. Twilight Zone   64
13. Into the Lion's Den   73
14. A Scientific Interlude   82
15. Number 70 Whitehall   85
     What is the Cabinet Office?   *85*
     Cabinet Office: Where is it?   *86*
     Cabinet Office: Origins of the Secretariat   *87*
     Cabinet Office: Lloyd George's Memoirs   *88*
     Cabinet Office: Ethos   *90*
16. Back to the Learning Curve   92

Contents

17. The Kitchen: People   97
18. The Kitchen: Parliament   109
19. The Kitchen: Civil Service   114
     Envoi   *118*
20. Last Port Before the Storm   120
21. The Quick Fix   124
22. The European Development Fund   131
23. Here We Go Again!   141
24. Back to Jerusalem   151
25. Through the Looking Glass   155
26. To Them That Hath Shall Be Given   167
27. The Heart of the Matter   173
28. Those Whom the Gods Wish to Destroy   178
29. The World Turned Upside Down   186
     Monetarism   *187*
     Privatization   *188*
     Trade Unions   *192*
     Efficiency in Government   *193*
     Relations with Ministers   *193*
30. À la Lanterne   199
     The French Civil Service Pay System   *201*
     Abolition of the Civil Service Department   *203*
31. The Labourer is Worthy of His Hire   206
     The Megaw Inquiry   *207*
     The Arbitration of 1982   *209*
     The Negotiations of 1983   *210*
     Index-Linked Pensions   *212*
32. Who Does What   215
     The Financial Management Initiative   *215*
     Grading   *218*
     The Dead Hand of Parliament   *220*
     Opening the Door   *223*
33. Into the Wild Blue Yonder   226

Index   227

List of Illustrations

1. A long walk under the gaze of the great man   6
2. Scratch eye Thursday   14
3. A stand-up desk of which Dickens would have been proud   20
4. Away went a star shell, unfused, to land in Reykjavik   24
5. Churchill used to dictate in his bath   42
6. Files started to move around at high speed   50
7. Winning by three broken bones to nil   58
8. The value of a Catholic upbringing   71
9. A spectacular experiment   84
10. An excited prime minister on the phone every five minutes   108
11. When the river burst its banks   118
12. A permanent reminder of the power of the negative   133
13. Who says the Civil Service can't do everything for itself?   145
14. To his credit Tony said 'go'   158

List of Illustrations

Photographs

1. The Rt. Hon. Baron Wilson of Reivaulx KG FRS,
   Prime Minister 1964–70 and 1974–76   93
2. The Rt. Hon. Lord Callaghan of Cardiff, KG,
   Prime Minister 1976–79   180
3. The Rt. Hon. Baroness Thatcher, OM,
   Prime Minister 1979–90   183

Acronyms and Abbreviations

a.k.a.	also known as
AP	assistant principal
ARP	air-raid precautions
BEA	British European Airways
BP	British Petroleum
BR	British Rail
BSE	bovine spongiform encephalopathy
CAP	Common Agricultural Policy
CBI	Confederation of British Industry
CIA	Central Intelligence Agency
CIEC	Conference on International Economic Cooperation
COREPER	senior official committee of ambassadors of member states to the European Community
CPRS	Central Policy Review Staff
CS	Civil service
CSD	Civil Service Department
CSSB	Civil Service Selection Board
c.v.	curriculum vitae
D-Day	Day Day
DGIV	EEC Competition Directorate
DSS	Department of Social Security
DTI	Department of Trade and Industry
EEC	European Economic Community
ENA	École Nationale d'Administration

Enarque	graduate of the École Nationale d'Administration
EU	European Union
Euratom	European Atomic Energy Community
FCO	Foreign and Commonwealth Office
FMI	Financial Management Initiative
GM	grant-maintained
GPO	General Post Office
HMG	Her Majesty's Government
IDC	industrial development certificate
IRA	Irish Republican Army
ISB	Iron and Steel Board
IT	information technology
K	knighthood
KGB	Komitet Gosudarstvennoi Bezopasnosti (Committee of State Security)
LCC	London County Council
LEA	Local Education Authority
LSE	London School of Economics and Political Science
Merc	Mercedes Benz
MINIS	ministerial information system
MoD	Ministry of Defence
MPO	Management and Personnel Office
NATO	North Atlantic Treaty Organization
NAZI	National Socialist German Workers Party
NCB	National Coal Board
NCO	non-commissioned officer
NEDDY	National Economic Development Office
NFU	National Farmers' Union
NHS	National Health Service
NUM	National Union of Mineworkers
OAP	old-age pensioner
OAS	Organisation de l'armée secrète
OECD	Organization for Economic Cooperation and Development

Ofwat	Office of Water Services
OPEC	Organization of Petroleum-Exporting Countries
PAC	Public Accounts Committee
PEO	principal establishment officer
PM	Prime Minister
PNQ	private notice question
PPS	parliamentary private secretary
PQ	parliamentary question
PR	proportional representation
Sabena	Société anonyme belge d'exploitation de la navigation aérienne (Belgian World Airlines)
SJ	Society of Jesus
snafu	situation normal, all fouled (*or* fucked) up
SNCF	Societé nationale des chemins de fer français
SOE	Special Operations Executive
S. of S.	Secretary of State
SS	Schutzstaffel (Nazi paramilitary organization)
stats	statistics
TU	trade union
TUC	Trades Union Congress
W-Day	wedding day
WRVS	Women's Royal Voluntary Service
WVS	Women's Voluntary Service (now WRVS)
yuppies	young urban (*or* upwardly mobile) professionals

Introduction

It is, I believe, the common experience of would be authors that the hardest labour lies in finding and agreeing the title of their new baby. The present work is a good example. It began life under the high tech name of *A Stroboscopic Life*; passed through a *risqué* phase when it was known as *Keep Your Pen Full and Your Bladder Empty!* (the advice given to new young committee secretaries before letting them loose on their first Whitehall meeting); changing tack again to a misquoted version of Thomas Carlyle's description of himself as 'a red tape talking machine'; and ending up with the final title of *Beautiful Ambiguities* which, besides being a quote from Harold Wilson also reflects the inherent nature of that type of political and official writing known in the trade as 'constructive' — namely based on the dictum 'Never under any circumstances tell a lie; but remember that you are under no obligation to answer unasked questions or to conduct a public striptease.'

The merit of the present title is that it, like much political waffle, is intriguing without being informative. The reasons for discarding the alternatives are many and various and range from a suggestion by my wife; through red tape being indissolubly linked in the public mind with bureaucracy (quite properly because it really existed — I have a genuine piece before me as I type); and that writing and talking are the tools of my trade (so, too, is thinking but some politicians and academics might get jealous if civil servants claimed this out loud). Moreover, I feel a close affinity with the irascible Mr Carlyle whose views of some of the parliamentarians of his day were trenchant ('windbags, weak in the faith of a God in whom they believe only at church on Sundays, if even then'). I wonder what he would have thought of the present generation?

As to the subsidiary part of this book's title (inside view and all that) I can claim an almost unique acquaintanceship with the inner working of the Whitehall machine. Among my earliest jobs in the service was a two-year secondment as a junior member of a Cabinet Office think-tank (the old 'economic section'). Later on I spent five years as a full-time Cabinet Office committee secretary (including three and a half years as head of the Economic Secretariat) — a post that involved attendance at almost all meetings of the Cabinet and its economic committees. In addition, I served at different times as the private secretary to a senior civil servant, as private secretary to a Cabinet minister and for three and a half years in Number Ten as the Prime Minister's private secretary in charge of home and parliamentary business. Add to this service at a senior level in the Civil Service Department, the Treasury and the Cabinet Office (Management and Personnel Office) and much involvement in the affairs of the European Community and the OECD and the whole shebang adds up to a large number of interesting learning curves.

The reader will notice that in all this activity there was precious little time for formal training. The armed forces were staffed (and no doubt still are) on the assumption that a percentage of their personnel would be absent at any one time on training courses. The civil service of my earlier years enjoyed no such luxury and had to rely on native wit coupled with a modicum of 'Sitting by Nelly' to get by. Luckily, as a generation, we had been conditioned to cope with most situations and I like to think that our hallmark was an earthy pragmatism. Of course we could have done with a good deal more training. And I am glad that my colleagues and I were able to play our part in filling this gap once the Fulton Committee presented its monumental report in 1968. My only fear now is that we may overdo training to the point where our staff elevate the theoretical over the practical — as some of our neighbouring civil services do. To be frank, the lawyer-ridden bureaucracy of Brussels with its intellectual arrogance, massive superiority complex, and practical incompetence, is an awful example of the Napoleonic legacy at its worst.

In chronological terms my life falls neatly into three parts. The first runs from my birth to my entry into the civil service at the age of 23. These were my very active formative years and may well form the subject of another chronicle when this one has been put to bed. The second period is dealt with in this present volume and covers my 34 years in the civil service to age 58. The third period — which could form the subject of a third volume if I survive long enough to write it — will deal with my adventures in the private sector and as a consultant to some rather unusual governments in the years since my 'retirement'. Those of you addicted to betting — and thus interested in my chances of survival — should know that I am already 16 years into the third phase and that my mother lived to be 94. Add to this a bypass and a pacemaker and I may well live forever.

The curious among you (as Harold Wilson once said 'Peter, that phrase is beautifully ambiguous') may care to know why this work takes the form it does. Basically, it is that I was always too tired/ busy/had better things to do than keep a diary. Of course I was also a law-abiding citizen and my employers expressly forbade me from keeping a day-to-day record of events or from tucking away the odd copy of interesting bits of paper. Nevertheless, with the help of published documents and other people's biographies and autobiographies, I have done my best to keep the facts straight. There are, however, limits to what can be achieved in this way and overall, while my recall is pretty good, names and dates are sometimes difficult to remember. Thus, while using some real names, especially of characters in the public eye, I have sought to spare my old friends blushes (and my own) by a bit of judicious ducking and weaving. The effect of this, coupled with the random nature of memory itself, is not unlike the flickering of strobe lights. Colour, light and rapid movements are all intermingled to spectacular effect but with more impression than shape; hence the nature of my book and its original title. As always, all errors and omissions are my responsibility.

Finally, I have to acknowledge my debt to my darling wife, Suzanne, for carrying three children, a house and me through many of the adventures chronicled here. I would never have made it without her.

OFFICIAL SECRETS ACTS

DECLARATION

To be signed by Civil Servants on appointment

My attention has been drawn to the provisions of the Official Secrets Acts, 1911, and 1920, which are set out on the back of this document, and I am fully aware of the serious consequences which may follow any breach of those provisions.

I understand that the sections of the Official Secrets Acts set out on the back of this document, cover articles published in the Press or in book form, and I am aware that I must not divulge any information gained by me as a result of my employment to any unauthorised person, orally or in writing, without the previous sanction of the head of the Department. I understand also that these provisions apply not only during the period of my employment but also after my employment in the Department has ceased.

Signed ....

Witnessed.......................................   Date ..22·8·49...........

xvii

1

Falling In

One afternoon in the spring of 1949 I walked up
Houghton Street and through the doors of the
Student's Union of the London School of Economics. At that stage of my life I had been a student at the LSE
for over two years after leaving the navy, and finals loomed
in the summer.

This is not the place for an account of my life in the preceding 23 years. Suffice it to say that my father was a
Guernsey man brought to this country as a boy by my
grandfather in the early days of the century; that I was one
of two boys in my junior school (as primary schools were
then known) to pass the eleven-plus; that I went thereafter
to an LCC grammar school; followed rapidly by evacuation,
the blitz, the Home Guard, the Air Training Corps, more
blitz (this time the high-tech sort with flying bombs and
rockets), work as a lumberjack and later as a farm hand, the
navy and, after demobilization, the London School of Economics. Us teenagers were kept pretty busy in the days before
TV.

But back to 1949 and the LSE union. As I sat down to
drink a cup of what passed for coffee in those days I noticed
a poster on the wall. It called for volunteers to try their
hands at a new way of joining the higher ranks of the civil
service. Called 'method two' the new method of selection
was based on the very successful work of the armed forces in

the latter years of the Second World War in sorting the wheat from the chaff in the ranks of would-be officer cadets. The War Office selection board was the prototype. The army's old First World War idea of selection was simple. Essentially, two questions sufficed. 'What school did you go to and were you in the OTC?' The prewar civil service had a more sophisticated version of this (after all, they needed people who could do more than simply die beautifully). In their system the prize of selection was earned by emerging from a very severe written examination in the top so many and then facing a very high-powered selection board. The snag was that the old way tended to produce clones of the existing members of the service. Moreover, the command economy built to run the war had perforce to recruit lots of strange people from business, the professions and academia, many of whom, despite being 'odd', had done remarkably well and some of whom were now in positions of power in the service. In addition, the ambitions of the new socialist government, backed by a massive majority at the polls, to create a new society would clearly need lots of folk to manage the transition and run the result. The old ways just would not serve unaided. (For those readers who did not live through it I can recommend two seminal works to give the unvarnished flavour of the age. These are Correlli Barnett's *Audit of War* and *The Lost Victory*.)

The poster led me to two reactions. First, I had passed the naval version of CSSB and had found it fun (I had particularly enjoyed being asked by a somewhat over-serious naval officer to make a speech about 'the most successful admiral in British history' and choosing Henry Morgan as my subject). The second reaction was one of anticipation at the thought of a short holiday in a country house at the government's expense. After all, as I lived at home, my ex-service educational grant for books, paper and the rest brought in little more than £2 a week. On this princely sum — and with some help from my indulgent parents and my own holiday earnings — I could, just, afford the occasional youth hostel, but country houses like Stoke D'Abernon Manor were out of my class.

In the event, the preliminary examination designed to whittle the crowd of applicants to a manageable number proved easy and in due course I found myself in the depths of leafy Surrey with a jolly bunch of companions. We were almost all ex-service males with an average age of about 23 and of the cynical disposition that was the hallmark of our generation. Frankly, we did not expect to pass. (After all, 'method one' was still churning out its classical Oxbridge clones and not much room we thought was left for us guinea pigs.) In short, and with the odd exception, we regarded CSSB as an interesting experience to be enjoyed in its own right but of no great intrinsic importance (a funny and not totally false impression of an establishment modelled on Stoke D'Abernon is to be found in A. P. Herbert's novel *Number Nine*).

The selection board itself followed and found it difficult to understand why anyone in their right mind should want to go (as I had said I did) to the Ministry of Town and Country Planning. Neither, in retrospect, can I, but at least it kept the conversation going. Even now, looking back, I find it hard to account for this curious ambition, which I can only put down to my own total ignorance of Whitehall, coupled with the prevailing propaganda, which, in the best Stalinist tradition, sought to divert our attention from pie on the table to pie in the sky (a.k.a. 'the New Jerusalem').

Finally, in August a letter dropped through my letterbox inviting me to join the Ministry of Fuel and Power as an assistant principal (an AP in the civil service jargon of the day) at the princely salary of £30 per month before tax and national insurance. Completely chuffed and in a state of blissful ignorance I dug my demob suit out of the wardrobe and set off to meet my fate.

2

The World of Work

As readers of my next book will know when I have written it my experience of work up to this point in my career — excluding school, university and the navy as not being 'real' work — was confined to various forms of manual labour. Put briefly, I had done quite a bit of farm work (including a continuous spell of several months), I had chopped down lots of trees for the Forestry Commission and I had worked part time behind a post office counter and full time delivering parcels at Christmas (including to Holloway Prison, which enabled me to boast to my peers that I had been both 'inside' and in a women's prison to boot).

On arrival at the ministry I was taken to see the principal establishment officer (a worthy nowadays no doubt known as the head of human resources but then universally known to his face as 'PEO' and behind his back as 'Sam'). He welcomed me to the Ministry, told me how overworked he was and explained the Ministry's training policy. Roughly put, his statement on training ran: 'You will be sent, when we can spare you, for a one week course run by the central departments (Cabinet Office and Treasury). They will put you in the overall picture.* There may also be the odd

---

* I went on this course about a year later. The talking heads were prestigious and included Sir Edward Bridges, the wartime secretary of the Cabinet who confounded us all by saying that his career was based on the accident of being in the right place at the right time.

chance to go on short courses on specific subjects but these are few and far between and your work here will always take priority.* The heart of your training, however, will be our policy of shifting new APs around from division to division every six months or so in order to give them experience in a wide variety of work situations.'

Most government departments at that time would, I think, have summed up their training policies in much the same way. To translate to modern American terms the policy was one of 'sitting by Nellie', or as the French, being realists, would have it, *'marche ou crève'*.

I was then taken by Sam to see the permanent secretary, Sir Donald Ferguson, who was a very small man sitting behind a big desk at the far corner of a large office. Visitors were thus faced with a long walk under the gaze of the great man to reach his citadel. If his visitor were important enough Donald would rise from his seat to greet them in the latter stage of their approach march. Otherwise, he would wave them to a chair facing his desk if his intentions were friendly and leave them standing if he wanted to intimidate them. As a conscious gesture of goodwill I was waved to the seat and sat on its hard front edge for the three minutes of interview granted to me. I cannot remember what Donald actually said but all my experience points to some variant on the theme, 'Welcome. Work hard. Keep your nose clean. Shut the door as you go out.'

---

* Some years later I was sent on a one-week course at York University on 'cost benefit analysis'. The main lesson I learned from this was the importance of the unintended consequences of well-meaning actions. The example given was that of a scheme to rationalize the distribution costs of electricity, water supplies and postal services in a rural community by concentrating scattered outlying farms into the heart of the village. New farms were built and the old ones abandoned only to be occupied later by townies as holiday homes. The newcomers promptly drank the water from the wells and died of bugs to which the old farmers were immune.

A LONG WALK UNDER THE GAZE OF THE GREAT MAN

Sam then took me back to his room in order to tell me two things. I was to be posted to the petroleum division on the overseas side. And my contract required me to work 24 hours a day, seven days a week and 52 weeks a year. If I were allowed to go home at nights and weekends, this leniency constituted an indulgence and a privilege bestowed on me as a favour by a soft-hearted employer and was by no means to be taken for granted.

So to my division, where a nice Welshman called Barry introduced himself as my boss. As I discovered later, Barry was one of the ex-members of the Indian Civil Service who had ended up in 'home' departments after independence. Now around thirty he had, in his early twenties, governed a territory containing over a quarter of a million inhabitants. In that job his superiors expected him to cope without running to them for guidance every five minutes — or every five months for that matter. He still ran a pretty independent ship.

I was shown to a desk and sat down waiting for something to happen, which it did very quickly. A knock on the door and a middle aged lady walked in. 'I'm so-and-so, come to take your subscription to the First Division Association. It represents your interests with management and everybody joins. Please sign this standing order to your bank.' I did so and almost immediately found a stream of visitors bound on similar errands of mercy. Within the hour I had subscribed to the Civil Service Benevolent Society, the Ministry's chess club, the football club, the dramatic society, the swimming club and one or two others I cannot now recall. Thus was I enrolled as a fully paid up member of the Ministry's social world.

And lest any readers should find this odd let me remind them that in 1949 the world outside work was a pretty cold place. The landscape in London and other major and minor cities throughout the land was dominated by bombsites — acres of mud decorated here and there by the odd static water tank and neat piles of recyclable bricks. Food was severely rationed — a misfortune only mitigated by the rations allocated to the Ministry canteen — an institution run, in the custom of the day, as a cooperative venture by the staff. Power cuts were frequent; public transport was crowded, dirty, sparse and stopped early; beer was weak and licensing hours short; pubs did not sell food beyond the occasional packet of crisps; restaurants were few and far between, as well as of doubtful quality; many theatres were shut as structurally unsafe and only the cinemas flourished — including, in London, a handful that showed foreign films. Oh the joys of Studio One, the Everyman, the Curzon and a few others of that ilk! And oh the hilarious, and very mild, naughtiness of Fernandel and his brothers and sisters in a world of censorship by, of all people, the Lord Chamberlain for theatres and the Hays Office for US films.

But for the most part we were thrown back on our own resources and the Ministry became our family — or a close rival to it — in a world, which, had we known it, had much in common with eastern Europe in its Marxist heyday.

3

New Colleagues

To the outsider the civil service looks homogeneous, staid, uniform and dull. Of course in the 1940s uniformity of clothing helped the illusion. Lowry's little men in black coats and flat caps existed in their hundreds of thousands, as did Giles's little men in bowler hats. But the cover of quasi-uniform hid a seething mass of separate individuals. Quite apart from the stratification of rank (which meant less and less as the greasy pole was climbed) several disparate groups could be discerned. The first and most important was the prewar intake, which in the late 1940s provided the generals and senior NCOs of the service who were, by then, the repositories of the Ark of the Covenant. They knew the rulebook by which we lived and what made the wheels go round in the real world. Many of them, moreover, were survivors of the First World War trenches and, in consequence, were as tough as old boots.

Another band of First World War survivors was formed of the large number of middle-aged ladies whose husbands or boyfriends had been slaughtered in France some 20 years before. In a world largely bereft of men they had had to fend for themselves. They, too, were tough and competent.

Yet another stream was of the lucky ones who had gone into the armed forces from the civil service in 1939 or 1940 before the system of manpower control got properly organized. Because, in law, they had simply moved from one branch of the royal service to another they continued to receive their civil service pay where this was higher than their forces pay. By and large they were the richest privates in the army and they used their wealth to pay others to clean their boots. Relatively few, if rumour was to be believed, bothered to seek promotion.

Next were the returning warriors from the Second World War. As already mentioned, we were a pretty cynical bunch, ready, willing and able to attribute the worst possible motives to our superiors, especially when they were politicians. As the Germans knew so well, servicemen keep sane by singing. But our songs were very different from the patriotic choruses of our German counterparts. Thus the Fourteenth Army in Burma marched to the strains of 'Betrayed by the country that bore us'; the RAF saluted its many dead with 'It serves him right he shouldn't have joined'; in Italy the brown jobs lamented that they were 'D-Day dodgers'; the army in Normandy rolled forward to the tune of 'They're digging up father's grave to build a sewer'; and the navy invented the supremely selfish 'I'm all right, Jack' — though in a much ruder version. Indeed, our capacity to mock authority was exceeded only by the inventiveness of our filthier songs from 'The ball of Kirriemuir' to the unauthorized version of '*Deutschland über Alles*'.

Finally, there were the boys and girls from school who crept into the service through the massed ranks of the ex-service and who had to compete with a generation whose c.v.'s had a wartime glamour about them. Thank heavens for the sociology department of LSE whose student body, although heavily permeated by ex-service entrants, was almost entirely female!

And within all these groups were the inevitable leavening of characters. Among the many I met was the undersecretary who rode to the office on a bicycle and whose first action on reaching his place of work was to hand his bicycle and bicycle clips to the messenger on duty at the front door.

Another, of similar rank, who, when it was raining, wore a 'ten-gallon' cowboy hat for protection. And then the newly demobbed army officer who put his army rank on the nameplate on his door (thus 'MAJOR BLOGGS') only to take it down very hastily when *his* boss put up one proclaiming 'LANCE-CORPORAL SMITH'. But sadder figures also stood out. There was the ex-SOE operative who had parachuted twice into occupied France and whose nerves had gone to pot (he left the civil service on the not entirely frivolous plea that he found it too exciting); and there was the young French woman who, so rumour had it, never went swimming because her back bore the scars of a Gestapo whipping. For all our cynicism, reality kept breaking through.

4

Early Lessons

Ut, to work it must be. My stay in overseas oil taught me a few basic lessons. Three weeks after I joined them the whole division, bar me, decamped to the USA for a conference with the Yanks. Before they left I did a lot of arithmetic as part of their briefing and, in the course of this, I used a calculator for the first time in my life. It was not, of course, electronic but of solid mechanical construction from Sweden. When my new masters had all left in search of their duty-frees, nylon stockings and the rest, I toyed with my Swedish steam engine and discovered to my horror that I had zipped when I should have zapped or whatever. In short, some of my painstakingly acquired numbers for the brief were wrong. I accordingly sent a humble telegram to Washington, which included the fatal phrase 'owing to error in calculator'. The response was swift and crushing. 'Calculators do not make mistakes only those using them do that.' In modern IT terms I had learned the basic lesson of 'rubbish in, rubbish out'.

The next, but far less painful lesson followed swiftly on the first. My undersecretary, Victor Butler — a cousin of the great Rab — took me as his bag carrier to a meeting of the programmes' committee. This was a committee of senior officials charged with the duty of allocating scarce import licences among the hungry departments ravening for them. The room was large; the throng was great (one reason for this was that the Treasury packed the benches with its own claque so that it could, it was alleged, shout down opposition to its views); the smoke cloud was thick (everybody, but everybody, smoked in those days); and the knives and knuckle-dusters were barely concealed. After a lot of talk, which passed over my head, we got to the item before ours. This was a modest request from the Ministry of Agriculture and Food for a licence to import £50,000 of bananas. The battle raged for half an hour. The Treasury line as I recall (and memory may well play me false, though I do not think so), was that 'what children did not know they would not miss'. The counter argument was that 'bananas were good for children' and anyway 'what about our starving colonies?' I am not sure but I think the softies won this one.

We then came to oil. 'Well Victor what do you think you'll need?' Smooth as silk came the answer 'About £400 million should do it I think.' To this the response was, 'that's OK then. Next item.'

The vital lesson for the new boy was that proper preparation for meetings pays dividends (one highly respected and successful company chairman told me much later that he tried never to go into a meeting without having prefixed the outcome). It also showed that speed is a vital component in a negotiating situation. The world is truly divided between the quick and the dead.

Finally, on the oil side, one of my chores was to go every month to the Bank of England to agree the estimates that would be part of the 'invisibles' component of the monthly balance of payments figures published by government. One day, when I arrived, my bank colleague led me past an office notice board with an expectant crowd around it. 'Odd', I said. 'What gives?' 'Oh,' he said, 'today is scratch-eye Thursday when the past month's merit pay awards are published for all to see. It's nice to get an award. It's murder when everyone is told you haven't got one'.

Many years later when I was responsible for the pay of the

civil service I bore this in mind together with the then belief of some major private companies that the strongest incentive effect of merit pay is achieved by putting a shroud of secrecy around the names of the recipients and the amounts they get. (I was told, for example, of one well-known company with a policy of secrecy on merit pay that found that it had far more staff members boasting to their mates that they received merit awards than actually got them — how's that for economy?) As it happened, I left the service before the present system was introduced, but I am willing to bet it is 'open' and under funded.

SCRATCH EYE THURSDAY

And, to move from merit to perks, one major oil company hired a permanent lunch table in a central London hotel for entertaining company guests. Inevitably, there were days when this table was not required and the convention had grown up that the young high flyers of the company could

use the facility, when spare, to entertain their contem-
poraries from business or government. Thus, I was introduced to what I once heard described as the 'smoked salmon
for lunch, boiled cod for supper' way of life. I also met some
20-year-olds who were to rise to fame later. For example,
Derek Ezra from the NCB later became chairman of that
institution and Peter Walters of BP became chairman of his
outfit.

To anticipate slightly, it is interesting that my next
encounter with the high life was in the realms of organized
labour. This happened when I joined the economic section
of the Cabinet Office (see next chapter). Among my colleagues there was a young man who eked out his civil service
pay by giving an occasional lecture to classes run by the
Workers Education Association. One day he asked me if I
could take on one such engagement, which he had been
offered but which clashed with a prior commitment of his.
The event was a summer school being run by a trade union
at a hotel in Bournemouth. I agreed with alacrity (who she?)
and was put in touch with the WEA organizer concerned.
Came the day and the organizer and I met at Victoria station. Shock one: 'Don't forget you need a first-class ticket.'
Shock two: 'Of course we'll have dinner on the train. It goes
on expenses.' Shock three: 'Let's get a taxi to the hotel. It's
quicker than a bus' and so on. Talk about the alternative
version of Labour's 'red flag' anthem. For those whose
education did not extend to this ditty, the key words are:

'The working class
Can kiss my —
I've got the foreman's job now.'

For the record, I also got an evening job lecturing in economics at the Regent Street Polytechnic. In those days it was
enough to know your subject to get work of this kind and I
kept up my connection with the poly until the uncertainties

of private office life made it impossible to continue. My time at the poly taught me two things:

- that preparing lectures means, at a minimum, keeping one chapter ahead of the class in their standard text-book; and
- that the ambitious young can still be very naïve. As witness to this I recall an evening when I explained to my class of budding bank managers that banks can lend a great deal more money than they possess and that, in effect, charging interest on non-existent money was the source of their pay and their shareholders' dividends. After the lecture was over I was approached by two of the audience who were most anxious to assure me that their banks could not conceivably act as I had described because to do so would be immoral.

5

The Posh End of the Business

Needless to say the planned six-monthly rotation among divisions did not take place. Instead, after a year of service in the overseas oil division I found myself packed off to the economic section of the Cabinet Office for a two-year stint. The section was a wartime hangover from the group of advisers in many disciplines that had been gathered around the war Cabinet and that was tasked to supply technical advice to the prime minister, other ministers and the many official committees that flourished at that time. The economic section I joined was headed by a noted Australian academic, Sir Robert Hall, and comprised a small band of ex-academics and serving civil servants with experience in economic affairs. It was housed in the Cabinet Office and enjoyed the prestige of being part of that organization. As a member of the section I also enjoyed the use of another wartime hangover, the Cabinet Office mess, which brought us into contact with the great and the good of Whitehall in an informal setting. Not that there was much fraternization, but at least we knew what they looked like.

On arrival it became clear that the reason for my transfer was that the Treasury had once again got its sums wrong. The pay offered for new recruits as economic assistants (which the section really wanted) was the same as that for APs and thus quite inadequate to entice the limited supply of good economics graduates to work for HMG. So the service had been trawled to uncover APs with economic training for temporary transfer as substitute economic assistants — hence my marching orders.

When I got to the section I found myself with four main tasks. I helped an economic adviser engaged in the negotiations to try and set up an international tin agreement (by devilling at home and not, to my regret, by travelling to Malaysia where much of the action took place); I acted as assistant secretary (the job not the CS rank of the same name) to the agricultural output committee — the official committee that handled the annual negotiations with the National Farmers' Union on the prices of home produced agricultural products; I sat in on the meetings of a fluctuating group of official committees of no great consequence as the 'statutory' representative of the section; and I played a major role in a piece of official machinery connecting the section to No 10.

The connection with No 10 is easily explained. All prime ministers receive copies of all papers circulated to ministerial committees so as to keep them and their staffs *au fait* with events in the boiler room. Clement Attlee and Sir Winston Churchill (the two prime ministers of my years in the section) were no exception. But, of course, no prime minister, however diligent, can read them all and their staffs are very busy. No doubt each prime minister finds his or her own solution to this problem. Clement Attlee's solution, continued after him by Sir Winston, was to commission the section to write succinct summaries of each such paper highlighting both the problem and the proposed solution or decision. This was a superb training exercise for the younger members of the section and its value was enhanced by the rigid rule that the maximum permitted length of the summary was half a side of a sheet of foolscap (near enough A4) paper. One line over the limit and the heartless private secretaries in No 10 would sling it back unread.

The job of assistant secretary of the agricultural output committee was fascinating and one for which, as a one-time agricultural labourer, I felt a particular affinity. The committee met intensively for several months of the year as backup to the annual negotiations with the National Farmers' Union on produce prices and market guarantees. The background was the emotional one of memories of near starvation in two world wars. This invested farming with a mystical quality that had little to do with practical reality but that was a very powerful political force. During the war the farmers had been told, with truth, that they, together with the merchant seamen who suffered such horrendous losses in bringing food across the Atlantic, were the saviours of the nation. Add to this the fact that farmers were disproportionately represented among the political classes and the stage was set for some high-class special pleading.

In all of this the attitude of the Ministry of Agriculture to the farming industry was one of total identification with its interests and objectives. The rest of Whitehall regarded the ministry as a branch office of the NFU but found the political weight of the department very difficult to resist. The department's success in looking after its clients persisted for a long time, with help in later years from the EEC's Common Agricultural Policy, until the mishandling of the BSE crisis of the past decade and the proposed expansion of the EU to the east brought the bandwagon to a shuddering halt. But in my days at the section the industry still rode very high indeed.

Modern readers will note with astonishment that, by the early 1950s, the UK alone among the Western members of the wartime alliance, was the only one still to ration food.

They may also note with astonishment that, when a senior member of the section developed a very painful back complaint, which effectively precluded him from sitting down, the squirrel tendencies of the (to Whitehall) notoriously inefficient Ministry of Works enabled them to find him a Victorian stand-up desk of a pattern of which Dickens would have been proud. Despite appearances, the Ministry of Works was not entirely useless.

A STAND-UP DESK OF WHICH DICKENS WOULD HAVE BEEN PROUD

And, of course, in the background the European Coal and Steel Community was created without British participation. As a very junior civil servant I was not privy to the reasons that led to our absence from Messina and Rome. But I can remember two attitudes that governed much Whitehall and Westminster thinking. The global issue was the inability of the Tory right to accept that the 'Empire' was no more. Vast amounts of treasure and some blood were spent on this illusion. But even the sucking away of the American loan from us by the rest of the sterling area did not cause the penny to drop. The fact that we had fallen rapidly in 1945 from the ranks of the victors to a second-class power on the fringe of the European continent did not register. Too many people around 1950 were to shun the idea of joining the 'club of the defeated' to make this a tenable political option. We were to pay dearly over the decades to come for this self-deception.

The second destructive attitude was the short-termism of the 'Gentlemen in Whitehall' who briefed the politicians. The message I heard rattling around the corridors of Millbank and the industries we, in the jargon of the day, 'sponsored', was all about 'dual pricing'. Shortages abroad and price control at home meant that the prices obtainable overseas for (as examples) coal, steel and iron and steel scrap were a good deal higher than those ruling in the home market. Consequently, home users of these products enjoyed a competitive edge over their foreign competitors. The fact that these advantages (in effect 'subsidies' from the coal, steel and scrap industries) would not last forever did not register: the fact that 'joining Europe' meant that they could not survive the signing of a treaty in favour of a free market did register. And putting both together meant that, in a chauvinistic view, grubby Europeans, many of whom had, 'we knew from our lads in Normandy', fought against us in the SS, were intent on snatching our competitive advantages away from us. And lest it be thought that I sympathize with this view, rather than simply recording it, I hasten to add that my wife's father, like her a French patriot, died gallantly fighting for freedom in the Maquis. And he was far from being alone.

6

The Dirty End of the Business

After my educative two years in the section I returned to the Ministry of Fuel and Power and was posted to our coal division. As it happened, the Ministry was about to embark on a consolidation of the safety in mines legislation, which was scattered over more than a century of miscellaneous law making and reflected everything from experience to bright ideas in the bath. In consequence, the safety law was in a real mess — a situation made worse by the habit of our ancestors of putting a host of detail into the primary legislation rather than, as now, into subordinate legislation. The point is that amending primary legislation is far more time consuming than bringing subordinate legislation up to date. In consequence, the old system tended to leave great swathes of out-of-date law lying about because no one could find the time, or the energy, to do anything about it.

My favourite example of the mayhem that old law can bring to the life of governments is the story of the Army Act. In 1688 the Glorious Revolution finally got rid of the Stuarts and in 1689 Parliament enacted the Bill of Rights which, among other things, provided that a standing army could only exist in peacetime with the consent of Parliament. This consent was subsequently granted annually so as to preserve parliamentary control. Thereafter, with the passage of time, approval became a formality with consent granted on the nod. In 1952, however, a few members of parliament led by the indefatigable George Wigg (who told me many years later that one of the great faults of Parliament was that too many MPs were 'too lazy to do their 'omework properly') actually read the legislation for which consent was sought. They then had great fun at the government's expense by demanding to know why this or that provision, designed for the seventeenth century, was not being applied in the twentieth. The upshot, apart from government blushes, was a parliamentary committee and a brand new act in 1954, which brought the law up to date.

Our old legislation was not of this catastrophic kind, being inconvenient rather than irrelevant. Nevertheless, tidying it up would greatly assist in the process of understanding and enforcement and thus was 'a good thing' and welcomed by the whole House. Within the division responsibility for producing the consolidated legislation was given to an assistant secretary (Grade 5 in the modern system) just returned from a sabbatical year in the USA on a Harkness fellowship. Dicky (as we all called him) looked like a caricature of a civil servant — black jacket, pinstripe trousers and all. But, beneath the veneer, was a romantic adventurer. I offer two facts in proof. First, he returned from the United States with an American wife whose accomplishments included being a top class player of the jazz trumpet. And, second, Dicky had served during the war as first lieutenant (second in command) of a coal-burning trawler that sought to defend Iceland from the ravening Hun. One night, while patrolling off the coast near Reykjavik, Dicky's lookout thought he saw a submarine on the surface some miles away. Forward rushed our gallant hero. 'Fire a star shell,' cried he. 'Bang' went the gun. And away went a star shell, fuseless, to land with a crash in the middle of Reykjavik, knocking a startled postman off his bicycle. In one quick moment Dicky became the only person on either side of the Second World War to shell Reykjavik — savage fellows these bureaucrats.

AWAY WENT A STAR SHELL, UNFUSED, TO LAND IN REYKJAVIK

While on the subject of wartime mayhem it is worth telling the story of a member of staff who had had a distinguished career as an officer of Royal Engineers in the Fourteenth Army in Burma. One evening we were both present at a reception for, I think, overseas civil servants come to London for a conference when my ex-engineer met a fellow engineer from Burma. The usual 'Have you been to Mandalay?' type conversation ensued. 'Do you know that marvellous building at X?' asked our Burmese friend proudly. 'I helped to build it.' 'Did you?' said my colleague thoughtfully. 'I blew it up.'

Before I get too far down the road of my narrative I ought, perhaps, to say words about the ethos of the civil service in the aftermath of war. It will already be clear to the two-thirds of my readers who were not born when the Second World War ended that the immediately postwar United Kingdom and its government and people were very different from anything they have known in their lifetimes. It is not my purpose to expound at length on the social and intellectual conditions that moulded the nature of our society in those early postwar years. Suffice it to say that we were, almost universally, poor, hungry and tired; that years of siege had ingrained an ideal of fairness in most of us; that years of shared endeavour, success and propaganda had bred an idealistic belief in our ability to achieve miracles; and that, in the background, was a strong feeling (rubbed home by, for example, the Gollancz yellow books) that our fathers' generation had been cheated of the fruits of their victory in the first war. In short, we were a generation that suffered, at one and the same time, from a sense of betrayal by our prewar politicians; from a total lack of realism about the realities of our diminished power in the world; and from a heady dose of idealism. Add to this a dangerous admixture of innocence, naïvety and cynicism and you will see a nation of crazy, mixed-up kids. In this situation some European societies went communist. Ours reverted to an earlier period of our history so that non-conformist, and indeed puritanical attitudes ruled the roost. The Old Testament was the part of the Bible that mattered (the concept of an eye for an eye was particularly favoured) and the ghosts of Oliver Cromwell's troopers stalked the land.

The civil service reflected, as always, the society from which its members were drawn. And it was a society that, while wanting to do good, could be very ruthless. Murderers were hanged without fuss. The American army in our midst hanged soldiers convicted of rape and no one thought it odd or excessive. The bombing of Dresden and Hiroshima raised a few eyebrows but the vast majority of the population regarded these events, not only as militarily justified, but as well merited revenge for acts of barbarism by the other side.

After all, in the last year of the war in Europe the concentration camps were being liberated and in the Far East the full horrors of the Japanese occupation, for example of the Philippines, were becoming apparent.

As a minor reflection of the age, one evening a night watchman patrolling my ministry came across a couple hard at it in an empty office. They were reported in the morning, seen by the permanent secretary straight away and sacked and out of the office before lunch. No one thought this out of the ordinary. They had taken a chance and lost. Tough!

But, back at work, my prime task of doing the research for the consolidation bill was to plough through all the old files to ensure that nothing was missed out. As a bonus, doing so gave me a bird's eye view of the working habits of our predecessors. The most impressive finding was the economy with which minor (and one suspects major) issues of policy were decided. A typical example from 1905 consisted of a simple cardboard folder containing two sheets of paper joined together by a treasury tag. The first sheet of paper was a letter from the Mineworkers' Federation of Great Britain to the minister saying, in effect, 'Clause X of your draft bill would be improved if you extended its scope to cover Y.' The outside cover of the folder had a string of short manuscript notes. The first was from the minister's private secretary to the official handling the bill saying, 'The Minister thinks this idea has merit but would be grateful for your advice.' The next was from the official to his boss saying, 'This is a sensible suggestion. We should accept it.' One more comment in similar vein from higher up the official hierarchy sent the folder back to the minister who added 'approved' and his initials. The second piece of paper was a letter from the private secretary to the union telling them of the minister's decision. The whole operation took about a week. No other department was consulted. In my day a similar operation would have generated at least an inch of paper and who knows how much Whitehall and outside consultation. And today the whole thing would be on a floppy disk containing the results of lots of electronic whizzing about. Moreover, of course, nowadays the disk would be sitting in a pending tray waiting for the responsible official to find time, in an impossibly busy life, to type his own letter to the union.

Incidentally, it was in this operation that I first came into contact with those real heroes of government, the parliamentary draftsmen. These are the very good and specialized lawyers who translate the wishes of government and Parliament into useable legalese. The point is that under our system the words in a statute mean precisely what they say and the courts assume (against all reason and experience) that Parliament knows what it is doing when it passes a draft text into law. For this system to work Parliament must know what it wants and be prepared to give the time and intellectual effort to expressing its wishes in clear English. Naturally this does not always happen but, in principle at any rate, the making of new law in the UK is built around devising a plain English statement of purpose and objectives and then giving this to the draftsmen to convert into precise legal language. Of course, no system can guarantee to eliminate human error but at least ours tries to ensure that as much light as possible is thrown into the thought processes of legislators by no means all of whom have legal training.

This matters because the means devised to make, or amend, laws are at the heart of the parliamentary process. Above all we should note that, unlike us, our Continental neighbours produce new law by starting from a draft legal text. This is then argued about and amended between ministries and politicians on its way to acceptance or rejection. A cynic might assume that the purpose of proceeding in this manner (and it was devised long before the EU was thought of) was precisely to stop democracy getting in the way of government. Indeed, it is not too far fetched to draw a parallel with the long use of the Latin Bible by the Catholic

Church and the liberating effect of the vernacular Bible when introduced into England and Germany. Perhaps an extreme case of the division of the legislative world into 'clerks' and 'proles' is to be found in the current practice of the Croatian parliament where officials are allowed to take part in the parliamentary debates on new laws so that the provisions can be explained and questions answered. The effect of this, therefore, is that a Croatian minister does not need to understand the law he is proposing in the way that, say, a British minister must if he is not to appear a fool to his fellow parliamentarians. I do not say that the present generation of Croatian ministers do not know their business. I just note that the system they inherited from their communist predecessors, and they in turn from societies infested by lawyers, had the result of keeping effective control of law making in non-democratic hands. The effect of the adoption of this practice by the EU is, one suspects, precisely to fool politicians both within the EU and in national parliaments. I leave it to others to judge whether this effect was intended. In doing so, I must declare myself an unreconstructed cynic where the elitist graduates of the École Nationale d'Administration or the École Polytechnique are concerned.

But let us look beyond the 'you are another' school of argument to what actually happens when the council of ministers (namely the ministers representing national governments) meet in Brussels to decide policy on a proposal put to them by the Commission. What they will have before them is a draft regulation or whatever giving effect to the Commission's proposal. This will already have been hacked over by working groups of officials culminating in a session of COREPER (the senior official committee comprising the ambassadors of member states to the Community). The version coming to ministers will be adorned with words and phrases in square brackets. Some will represent alternative texts (with 15 member states theoretically up to 15 of them); others will represent yes or no choices each backed by a group of member states. The chairman will then take the meeting stolidly through the text, square bracket by square bracket. Some brackets will have been dealt with in pre-meeting bargaining; others will be settled by qualified majority voting where this applies; yet others will be remitted for further consideration either at a later meeting or by small groups meeting in parallel with the main meeting; and yet others, again, will send the meeting off into a flurry of instant drafting by those present. To get the full flavour of this latter process imagine a drafting party of 15 people each with an axe to grind and operating in a variety of different languages through a fog of simultaneous translation of variable quality. As Samuel Johnson said of a dog walking on its hind legs, 'It is not done well; but you are surprised to find it done at all.' Just think if we had joined in the beginning we might have led our neighbours into the paths of democratic (and Anglo-Saxon) righteousness and control of over-mighty employees. As it is we (and the EU) are stuck with a system of decision taking designed to entrap the unwary, the slow and the amateur (which some might think is a good description of a number of British ministers and their aides).

But that is enough of digression. We need to get back to coal. At the time when I had a hand in the coal scene the industry had already been nationalized. The reality of that act of social progress was that an industry long dying of under-investment had been flogged to near ruin during the war. Two things alone could save it: massive capital investment (which could not be raised from private sources because the risks were too high); and a revolution in the attitudes of the labour force to productivity and restrictive practices. Nationalization provided the money by forcibly taking it from the taxpayer. Despite initial delusion, however, socialism did not change the attitudes of the men or of their unions. I remember arguing with an old school acquaintance, who was a dedicated communist, that nationalization removed any reason that may have existed for lack of cooperation between men and management. He vehemently denied this. In his view (or rather in the view of the party line he parroted) nationalization within a fundamentally capitalist society was a sham. The whole of society had to be changed before the golden age could begin. It was around that time that (with the aid of Arthur Koestler and similar writers) it finally dawned on me that the missing element in his description of the communist line was brute force.

A small story may help (inadequately) to illuminate the coal industry's attitudes at this time. In the immediate postwar years British industry in general, and the coal industry in particular, suffered from a severe lack of managerial talent. This lack was compounded in the nationalized industries by the harsh restraint on the pay of their senior management imposed by ministers at the behest of the TU part of 'this great movement of ours'. Add to this the penal rates of income tax in force at the time and it was not surprising that the Treasury's favourite source of recruits to nationalized industry boards was the mass of newly retired admirals, generals and the rest thrown up by the demobilization of our armed forces — if only because the continued payment of their forces' pensions reconciled them to the Treasury's miserliness. (Actually, the main source of the trouble was ministers, not the Treasury, with Tory ministers remembering what they paid their gardeners and Labour ministers tied to the carriage wheels of the mass unions of the low paid and their own propaganda.)

The story goes of one general newly appointed to a senior management post in the coal industry who went underground for the first time. When he saw some miners shovelling coal onto a conveyor belt he seized a shovel and joined in (no doubt remembering his training in man management). The following conversation ensued with his miner neighbour:

Miner:	'Art tha' a member of t'union?'
General:	'No.'
Miner:	'Then put down that f------ shovel.'

Another truth illustrated by a canny member of the NCB when asked how long a particular industrial dispute would last: 'a long time. Don't forget there are bloody minded Yorkshire men on both sides of the negotiating table.'

A standard technique for mining coal with explosives is called 'shot firing' — where sticks of dynamite or some similar explosive are put in the exposed coal face and 'fired', thus bringing down the coal for loading into a tub or onto a conveyor belt. For many years the rumour persisted that an early annual report of the NCB contained the classic typo 'shit firing'. I could never find it but am sure a fortune awaits anyone who can. Incidentally, this story illustrates the vital importance of the very dull chore of conscientious proof reading of government texts.

On a different issue, the coal division gave me my first opportunity to travel abroad at the taxpayer's expense. I went to the Ruhr on an exchange visit with the German Ministry of Economics and found myself making my very first trip underground (ever) in a German coal mine. Having seen that splendid pre-Nazi German film about coal miners *Kameradschaft*, I found the mixture of overt friendliness and a slight whiff of military discipline quite familiar. I was also intrigued by the local custom of continuously saying '*Gluck Auf*' to every fellow being met underground. Did it mean, as the miners seemed to imply, 'I wish you a safe journey to the top' or did it mean 'You'll be lucky to get out of this place'? Or was it just that English has more nuances than German? I never did find out. I also met an ex-member of the *Waffen* SS who drove me from one appointment to another. Two phrases he used stick in my mind: 'I wish I could show you the cine film I shot in Russia. Shells bursting just in front of my camera;' and, after asking what branch of the armed forces I had served in and being told the navy, responding with, 'that was an honourable service.' (I think he suspected I had been a bomber pilot or *Terrorenflieger* as the Germans dubbed them. It all depends where you are sitting when the bombs fall down.)

And I should mention one mechanical point. Just as the Treasury did not pay enough to recruit economic assistants so it tried to recruit scarce typists on the cheap (and outside London by single, national rates of pay). This was OK in the frozen north where local talent was available but no go in the south. Those of us without personal secretaries had a choice of sending manuscript drafts for typing 'up north' (in our case to Lytham St Anne's) and taking our chance on the timing and quality of the finished product, or of bribing our bosses' secretaries with charm or chocolates. Negotiating with the EEC or the NUM was a doddle after that.

7

First Link with the Internet

By 'internet' here I do not mean the modern electronic gizmo but the web of personal relationships that make the wheels of any organization go round. There are a number of such networks in Whitehall but the one that really matters is the one that links the private secretaries of ministers and senior officials to each other and to the Cabinet Office secretariat. Subsidiary but important service-wide nets are those linking the personal secretary-type secretaries of the great and the good and those provided by the chauffeurs of the government car service. The latter are the prime source of Whitehall's best rumours (their passengers tend to ignore them like wallpaper). The other two are fixit arrangements of considerable power.

Before going further I should explain for the benefit of the non-civil service reader that the postwar civil service (other than the Ministry of Defence, which was always a law unto itself) had relatively few chiefs to look after a very large number of Indians. In the Ministry of Fuel and Power, for example, we had several thousand staff in total and only three officials in the two highest grades (one permanent secretary and two deputy secretaries). After the fashion of the day all three had knighthoods (the then Treasury's preferred substitute for cash) and, more to the immediate point, all three had assistant principals as their private secretaries. These appointments had two purposes — helping with the work and learning one's trade in sitting by some high-class 'Nellies'.

The gentlemen concerned naturally also had the help of a 'real' secretary and one or two clerks. In 1952 I found myself appointed as private secretary to one of the deputy secretaries — a certain Sir Lawrence Watkinson — among whose claims to fame was that of being a survivor of four years of infantry warfare in France. In a word he was, like other similar survivors, a very crafty, educated killer from whom I learned much.

Indeed, learning how the wheels really go round was three parts of the job. In it I saw almost every piece of paper that came across my boss's desk. As a member of the economic section I had, of course, already had an unusual exposure to Cabinet committee papers for one so young. But in my new job I enjoyed the full Monty. Papers, minutes (or conclusions as the Cabinet minutes, alone of those of all ministerial committees are known — presumably to show there is no higher court of appeal), letters, telephone conversations (always monitored unless personal), note taking of meetings in the office and so on and so on. In short, I was in possession of almost all the information available to the second in command of a ministry and I watched him digest it and act on it. This was more than sitting by Nellie. It was a ringside seat in a very active playhouse.

In addition to the ride on a very steep learning curve, a few key memories highlight the man as well as the job. Thus, Wattie picking up the phone to answer a barrage of abuse from a disembodied voice, listening for a few seconds and then cutting in with 'I will continue this conversation when you have recovered your manners' and slamming the phone down. I am not absolutely sure but I am pretty certain that the caller was a minister. But, having seen off the Kaiser's army, I suppose that ministers come easy.

Next, Wattie was invited to take on the chairmanship of the ministry's Sports and Social Council and enjoyed imposing his own distinctive management style on that ancient body. To explain, the council was one more hangover from the war with members drawn from the Ministry's sports and social clubs across the country. Among other things, it played a part in disbursing the very meagre sums of money allocated to staff recreation in our budget. Before Wattie (BW as we should have thought to call it) its meetings had been a paid day out for the delegates. Sir Lawrence's first meeting changed that. 'I have worked it out, he said, that this meeting is costing the taxpayer £X a minute. The sooner we get back to work the better.'

Again there was Wattie sending for an undersecretary who was to chair an interdepartmental working group on a subject he regarded as none of their business and delivering the following instructions: 'You are now going to chair a wholly impartial review of X. I have jotted down on this bit of paper the conclusions I expect you to reach.'

Finally, the reader will have noticed that three of the four members of staff in our office had job descriptions incorporating the word 'secretary' — one deputy secretary, one private secretary and one secretary. This is, therefore, as good a point as any to comment on the confusing habit of the then British civil service and government in overusing the job title of secretary. (It has got a little better since but not much.) Think of it. There is secretary of state, permanent undersecretary of state, permanent secretary, deputy secretary, undersecretary, assistant secretary, parliamentary secretary, principal private secretary, private secretary, parliamentary private secretary and, of course, just plain secretary. In addition, the confusion extends overseas. For example, with us a secretary of state is a senior minister. In Germany and a number of other countries a state secretary is the official in charge of a government department. Add to this the fact that, for us, a government department is a ministry (as indeed it is in the USA) whereas in many countries a department is a subunit of a ministry. Try explaining that to a multinational committee, meeting after lunch, with inadequate translation facilities, or even with them.

As a postscript to all this talk of work I must record one very personal kindness by my boss, which went a bit wrong but left an indelible impression. Wattie was a very keen fisherman and each summer he set off to catch salmon in remote highland rivers. It must have been in 1953 that he sent his personal secretary (who had worked for him for years and was the only person in the ministry allowed to swear at him) and me a magnificent specimen of that glorious race of fish (which incidentally was very expensive in those days). Unfortunately, the GPO was up to its usual trick of striking for no very good reason that I could discern and the crucial parcel got delayed on its way south. By the time it reached us it stank. Nevertheless, we knew that the old man (being in his late fifties he seemed pretty ancient to both of us) was very proud of his fishing skills and we did not wish to hurt his pride. So we both put on an act. 'It was delicious' we lied. Even this little drama was, I suppose, part of my training for the world of politics I was now about to enter.

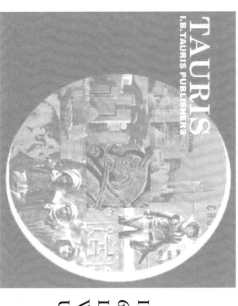

TAURIS
I.B. TAURIS PUBLISHERS

I.B. Tauris & Co Ltd
6 Salem Road
London
W2 4BU
United Kingdom

Please add my name to your mailing list to receive details of books in the following subject areas

Middle East ☐   Archaeology & Ancient History ☐   Asian Studies ☐
Islamic Studies ☐   Art & Architecture ☐   Central Asia ☐
Iran ☐   Film / Media / Visual Culture ☐   Human Geography ☐
Jewish Studies ☐   Politics, Intl. Relations & Defence ☐   Modern History ☐
Women's Studies ☐   Russia & Former Soviet Union ☐   African Studies ☐

My other areas of interest are:...

Name...

Address...

....

....

Postcode.......................... Email address.......................... Date..........

Your requests can also be directed to marketing@ibtauris.com

8

Closer to the Centre

In 1954, after two happy years as a sorcerer's apprentice, I was moved to the minister's office (known as the private office in Whitehall jargon — presumably because most of them look like a main-line railway station during the rush hour). The private office is the working hub of the ministry and, as an assistant private secretary to the minister, that is deputy, stand-in and general factotum to the private secretary proper, I had moved closer to the centre of power. The task of the two of us, aided by a small but expert staff of clerks and typists, was to achieve four basic objectives. First, we had to ensure that the minister arrived on time, in the right place, clutching the right papers and properly briefed, at all his engagements including his parliamentary engagements (the Cabinet Office mantra for this was to ensure that a member or secretary of a committee arrived at a meeting 'with his/her pen full and bladder empty'). Second, we had to manage his timetable (a task we shared with his personal staff). This split between, essentially, the official and personal/political sides of a minister's life can be very difficult to manage. We were lucky because, unlike some others, we had very good and friendly relations with our private counterparts. But achieving a good working relationship can take a deal of tact, which is not given to everyone (even in the world of *Yes Minister*).

We also had to act as the interface, both ways, between

the minister and the department. Of course, senior officials were the ministers' advisers and we did not seek to usurp their role (this can happen but almost invariably ends in tears). But ministers and officials have, quite properly, different agendas and priorities, as well as speaking different versions of the English language. The reality is that any good private secretary can greatly ease the processes of decision taking by explaining the needs and wishes of the two groups to each other. Again ministers have, or should have, an appetite for facts. Private secretaries can provide these or, more usually, can arrange for them to be provided. Indeed, in my experience the most important attributes of an effective private secretary are knowledge of the right button to push to get expert advice and the ability (and sometimes the courage) to say 'I don't know, but I will find out' rather than guess the answer to a factual question. (And the careful ones check their answers anyway just in case.)

Finally, the private office is the main channel of communication between the ministry and the Cabinet Office and the minister and his colleagues where collective business is at issue. The business concerned is not so much policy — others negotiate that — but procedure, where again the Cabinet Office has an aphorism for it: 'get the procedure right and the policy will follow.'

To return to my co-conspirator, Noel had had an exciting war as the pilot of a Lysander spotter aircraft. As such, he was one of the intrepid bands of flyers whose main job it was to potter about over the German front line correcting the aim of our artillery. Meanwhile, of course, the Germans, who quite sensibly did not like being fired at, did their best to shoot them down. And these were the easy jobs. The hairy ones involved carrying characters like our ex-SOE colleague into France in the middle of the night and hoping to God that the shadowy figures lurking on the fringes of the drop zone were not fully paid up members of the SS.

But Noel's real claim to fame was as the man who invaded

Wales. It arose like this. Early on the morning of D-Day, when it was still dark, Noel took off to fly to Normandy where it was hoped that some equally nutty characters would have seized a small field, ejected the resident cows and got all ready to greet him. He would then be launched again skywards to resume his normal career of playing gooseberry to the *Wehrmacht*. Unfortunately, Noel got lost and blundered about in the morning mist looking for the Continent (which in the classic words of *The Times* was 'isolated' by the weather). Eventually, through a gap in the clouds, he spotted not only the sea but some land as well. By this time he was running out of both fuel and patience and landed on the first available open patch of turf. A figure rushed at him out of the darkness clutching a large rifle with an even larger bayonet on the end of it. Incomprehensible jabberwocky came from the excited figure. Noel promptly started to rummage through the detritus of long forgotten French and German lessons that lurked in the dustier corners of his mind. Having dismissed such useful phrases as '*Madame Mercier est une femme*' and '*Guten Morgen gnadige Frau*' as perhaps a trifle inappropriate to the circumstances, it suddenly dawned on our intrepid hero that the language of his captor was Welsh. A few moments later, Noel and Taffy were happily agreeing with each other that France was 'thataway' and the local constabulary was organizing a supply of petrol from a nearby RAF base. In due course, I am happy to say, Noel arrived in France and the British army was enabled to resume the war.

At the time I joined the private office our minister was Geoffrey Lloyd. His main claim to fame was that he was the leader of the Tory party in the Midlands and spent much time on party business in Birmingham and adjacent parishes. His second claim to fame was that he was filthy rich and, by repute, was the most eligible bachelor for miles around. I am not qualified to comment on this latter claim but if a house in Belgravia and a new Bentley delivered to the door every summer signify anything I will readily concede his wealth.

One of his other claims to fame was that, way back before the war he had been a parliamentary private secretary (PPS) to Mr Baldwin. I never did know what side he had been on over Munich but promotion by Mr Churchill was normally a sign of being a 'goody'. You may wonder how this sort of miscellaneous information came my way. It arose from the 1956 general election in which Geoffrey was inevitably a candidate. One day he brought his newly printed election address to the office to show us. The photograph showed a smiling Geoffrey looking about thirty years old (he was getting on for sixty at the time) and dressed in clothes of an old fashioned cut. A cautious query 'Gosh, who took that photo?' got the reply that it had been taken in the days when he had worked for Baldwin and he saw no reason to discard a picture that had served him well over the years.

Oh yes, we must not forget Geoffrey's mum. She was a formidable lady in her eighties who kept house for her bachelor son. The trouble was that she had little idea of how ministers' mums are supposed to behave and none whatever of the importance of ministers. To illustrate, one day Geoffrey failed to turn up at the office and his driver reported that he had called to collect him at his home but had been told by the old lady that 'the minister would not be coming to the office today'. Shortly afterwards, Geoffrey telephoned in some dudgeon to ask where his car had got to because he was still waiting for it. When he eventually arrived we learned that the minister had awoken with a cold and his mother had decided off her own bat that he needed a day at home to recover. The trouble was that she did not tell him but had simply turned off the switches on her own.

There are a few more stories about the realities of power and then I must get back to work. In the normal course of business private secretaries sometimes take work to their bosses at home. And in the chunk of the corporate state the

Conservatives had inherited from the postwar Labour government, appointments to nationalized boards, including all
their regional boards and sundry advisory committees took
up a lot of ministerial and official time. We in the Ministry
of Fuel and Power were responsible for upwards of 500 such
appointments (including, it was alleged, one advisory committee in Wales every member of which was named Evans).
One consequence of this cornucopia of jobs was the need for
every potential new appointee to receive a formal offer
letter, and later a formal letter of appointment, from the
minister. Such letters were tailor made for being carried to
the minister for signature at home by junior private secretaries. Thus, one day I arrived at the front door of the
minister's Belgravia home, rang the bell and was admitted to
the house. His mother said 'He's upstairs. Excuse me if I
don't come with you but you will be able to find your own
way.' Up I then went, conscious that I knew nothing of the
internal geography of the house. But all was well. The
minister heard me coming and called out 'I'm in here. Please
come in.' In I went to find my boss sitting up in his bath.
'Hello,' he said, 'Churchill used to dictate in his bath. I've
always wanted to do something similar at least once. What
work have you got for me?' It made a change.

Next, another story illustrates the strength and ingenuity
of the private office network. In 1954 the US mid-term
congressional elections attracted a lot of political attention.
In the middle of the campaign the minister decided that he
needed to send a party representative to the USA at once to
watch the campaign and report. However, he rapidly
discovered that in the world as it then was a simple
operation like flying to the USA required traversing a
bureaucratic minefield. He therefore asked for our help. The
situation was that our friend had no ticket, no airline
booking, no US visa, none of the necessary medical jabs and
no US currency (the export of which was tightly controlled).
It was also a Saturday morning when the civil service of

those days worked but much of the rest of the country did not and ideally the representative should fly to the States that night. The minister, or the party, would pick up all the costs but it was up to us to make it happen.

CHURCHILL USED TO DICTATE IN HIS BATH

In the event it worked. The FCO private office conjured a visa out of the US embassy by using magical methods known only to them; the government's chief medical advisor was persuaded by his minister's office to give the relevant inoculations (we gathered that he was in fact tickled pink to revive a medical skill unused for 20 years and we all hoped it had not hurt too much); the Ministry of Civil Aviation got a ticket and a booking from British Overseas Airways (which in those days was no mean feat); and the Treasury raided the reserves to find a handful of tattered greenbacks. The subject of all this attention must have felt like a parcel as he was whisked by taxi at breakneck speed from one appointment to the next. But he caught his plane and we congratulated ourselves on having a bunch of friends around Whitehall who were prepared to help us, and indeed to go to a great deal of trouble for us, on the strength of a telephone call.

Even in the 1950s new technology struck. One day, electricians arrived and announced that they had come to install a new telephone system. Much flourishing of wire and wire cutters ensued and we were given a book of instructions. The essential difference was that we now had a mini switchboard concentrating all the lines coming into the office in one box. This was great. Now we would know which phone was ringing (a little light would flash) and we could more readily carry out our twin functions of getting the right person to the phone and listening in to the calls that mattered. And, to avoid misunderstanding, the listening function was not designed to entrap the unwary but to make sure that any commitments the minister made were recorded so that action could be taken to carry them out. Or, as sometimes happened, any incoming news for the department could be jotted down so that its onward transmission should not be overlooked.

But, in addition to the switchboard, we had also acquired a new toy — a recording machine, which, we were assured, would enable us to record telephone conversations so that no subsequent dispute could arise over who said what, to whom, when. This machine worked on what were the first genuine floppy discs. They were made of a sort of plastic paper and really did flop about. There was, I remember, some dispute about the ethics of these machines. Should we tell people that their voices were being recorded or no? In the end the caution of old soldiers and sailors overcame our qualms and we decided to see whether the bag of tricks actually worked before stirring up a hornet's nest of irresolvable moral issues. Not entirely to our surprise a trial run showed that while a reasonable, if faint, recording was produced of what was said at our end of the wire, the other end was just a jumble of crackling noises of no use to either the KGB or us. After various unsuccessful attempts by the engineers to improve matters, we were able, with a sigh of amoral relief, to revert to pencils and bits of paper as the principal tools of our trade.

Talking of the KGB it was around this time that Messrs Bulganin and Khrushchev, in effect the joint rulers of the Soviet Union, came to London on an official visit. Their itinerary included a courtesy call on our minister and I, and most of the rest of the ministry's staff, hung out of the windows overlooking our main entrance on Millbank. The scene was astonishing. Security required that the public be held back from the stretch of road between the office and the river. In their place two lines of security men were drawn up on either side of the road facing inwards. Those on the riverside pavement were British — as evidenced by their uniform dress of duffel coats and flat caps — and those on the near side of the road were KGB, all wearing identical long black overcoats and trilby hats. To film buffs like me the scene was set for a Mack Sennet comedy with the two lines of Keystone cops shooting each other down as the big black cars swept up the middle of the road and the principal actors ran for the shelter of the doorway. In the event the visit went well, though we were intrigued to learn later from one of the British security men that by leaning out of the window we had been in danger of being shot by the Russians who were always on the lookout for would-be assassins.

Oh yes, right at the beginning of my stint with Geoffrey he was holding a meeting in his room and I was fending off unwelcome or unprogrammed visitors in the outer office when the phone rang. It turned out to be No 10 with an urgent message for the minister. I cannot remember what it was about so it cannot have been all *that* world shaking, but No 10 was No 10 so I dashed into the room next door, excused myself for interrupting and gave the news to

Geoffrey. He thanked me and then drawled out the unforgettable words 'Next time, Peter, slowly. Like a policeman going to an incident.'

Talking of policemen, the minister's driver usually parked the official car around the corner in a side street. One day all the places there were taken (which shows what a different world it was) and he parked outside the front door on the main road. Along came a bobby and said, 'You can't park here.' 'But I am the minister's driver and this is his official car,' said the driver. 'All the more reason for him not parking here,' said the policeman. 'He made the bloody laws. He'd better obey them.'

Incidentally, we always addressed our ministers as 'Minister'. Most of them addressed us by our Christian names. The other kind exists in all parties. Neither the doctrine of 'one nation' nor that of 'the brotherhood of man', or of whatever the Liberals believe in, stops all governments from containing arrogant snobs, which is as far as I intend to take this subject.

The Ministry of Fuel and Power was essentially a device for controlling and financing the nationalized fuel industries — coal, gas and electricity — and for helping the oil industry to navigate profitably through a very difficult world to the national benefit. Three points are of interest. One, the Scots were happy to have local control of the gas and electricity industries but would not touch coal with a bargepole. They are not called 'canny' for nothing. Two, the nationalized industries impinged on the national economy at three points — prices, pay and taxes — and their influence on each was, on balance, malign. And three, given the dominating role of the mining unions in the Labour Party and the sheer size of the mining labour force (about three-quarters of a million men in 1950) the ministry operated willy-nilly in a political minefield — in many ways akin to that of the Ministry of Agriculture although with a different political orientation.

Finally, as already indicated, a major portion of ministerial time in the department was spent in trying to find people to run the many facets of the corporate state that lay in our bailiwick. Particular difficulty attached to finding chairmen for the boards. Looking at the problem from the perspective of a lifetime's association with the nationalized industries, and not just from the worm's eye view of Geoffrey Lloyd's office, our chairmen divide into distinct categories. As I have already mentioned, in the early postwar years the labour market was awash with youngish retired generals, admirals and so forth. They had two big attractions. They had run large organizations (albeit with the aid of highly trained staffs) and, because they had pensions, they could be hired relatively cheaply. The fact that, for the most part, they knew nothing of trade or commerce did not matter in those innocent days. A bit later on we had chairmen drawn from a wide variety of backgrounds including the career ranks of the industries concerned (on the questionable grounds that they at least knew what they were doing). Among these were the engineers and scientists who always faced the temptation of playing super-Meccano with other people's money. But until the advent of Maggie Thatcher, and a proper understanding of the labour market, not least by the Treasury, we continued to have great difficulty in hiring the requisite talent. Of course there were honourable exceptions — Dr Beeching springs to mind — but failure to recognize the validity of the aphorism that 'if you pay peanuts you get monkeys' led to a considerable amount of the nation's wealth and potential being squandered.

Before leaving this subject (and the private office) I must mention another very successful chairman of a nationalized industry — Sir Walter (later Lord) Citrine — who was an ex-leader of the TUC and chairman of the Central Electricity Authority. Most of our chairmen treated their ministers at the latter's own valuation, namely with due deference. Walter Citrine did not. A message to his office that the minister wanted to see him urgently received the reply, 'Tell him I'm free next Tuesday afternoon if he cares to call in at my office around four o'clock.' And another request for him to take some particular line of action received the crushing reply, after, I was told, riffling through the statute setting up his organization, 'I don't see where this gives him the right to ask me that.' In saying this, Citrine was echoing a common (private) complaint of board chairmen that ministers of all parties tried to use extra-statutory persuasion rather than open requests to make their nationalized industries toe a politically convenient line. The real trouble, of course, was that too few chairmen were prepared to say 'Put that in writing and I'll consider it.'

The fuzziness of the relationship between ministers and nationalized industries in the UK is now largely a matter of history, but it is interesting to note that in Sweden almost all communications between their state industries and government are available for public scrutiny. Moreover, their industries, and the agencies that run so much of their government machine, have their duties spelled out in statute law (so that questions of jurisdiction are for the courts to decide) and have trade unionists, businessmen and MPs of all parties on their controlling boards and committees. When the British government adopted the agency system for managing wide swathes of the public service in recent years these key features of the Swedish template were omitted.

There is one point to add before we move on. Although my duties were essentially to support the private secretary I also carried full responsibility for dealing with all mail from MPs and the public and for handling all parliamentary questions. In doing this I learned a lot. For example, I saw one minister who had given a wrong answer to a PQ (as a result of a departmental snafu) who had, by the then conventions of the House, to stand up and apologize for his error in what is known as a personal statement at the end of question time. His obvious discomfiture was reinforced by the tradition of the House of hearing such statements in total silence. The official who let that one through must have been a very unhappy bunny.

Letters also presented problems for the drafter (though with rather less risk of catastrophe because there are no instant supplementaries). Provided that the golden rule of textual accuracy is observed (never knowingly tell a fib) letters, like PQs, do not require a full confession. The questioner is responsible for his question and cannot complain if it is answered as put. However, the real problem with letters was one of style not substance and the older members of the department were set in their ways. In the result, many of the draft letters were couched in the jargon of a bygone age. It was very early in my days with Geoffrey that he brought me up against the realities of official correspondence when he reacted to one particularly stuffy draft with the phrase, 'I can't write to X like this. He's a friend of mine.' So from then on I made sure that the drafts that came across my desk were, in today's jargon, 'user friendly'. Of course there is no pleasing everyone so I was not surprised to receive a message from one undersecretary whose draft I had altered, 'I only hope, Le Cheminant, that when you leave private office you are posted to my division.' Luckily, I wasn't so posted. Luckily, too, all this experience was to stand me in very good stead in the years immediately ahead.

9

Lies, Damn Lies and Statistics

At the turn of the year 1955/6 I was promoted to principal (grade seven in today's system) and posted to our statistics division. As with my earlier posting to the economic section of the Cabinet Office I was sent to this job because the Treasury could not, or would not, compete in the market for professional staff — in this case statisticians — and my omnibus LSE degree included a subsidiary paper in statistics. I am not sure whether the Treasury knew that we LSE graduates called this paper a course in 'how to mislead with statistics'. (I suspect that they did and were well versed in the techniques concerned.)

My boss in this job was an ex-actuary originally employed by the Admiralty. He was a kindly man who ran an insurance business on the side and who possessed a magnificent 'feel' for numbers. He taught me a great deal. The first lesson came early on when he commented on a paper I had written that it was good but he did feel that papers from the statistics' division should contain at least one number. Thereafter, I kept a pepper pot of numbers handy and scattered them around with great liberality.

Another key lesson was my mentor's story of his Admiralty days when Whitehall got one of its periodic fits about measuring its productivity. In the Admiralty's case someone came up with the splendid wheeze that a measure of clerical productivity could be found by recording the number of times case files passed from hand to hand. No sooner said than done and a system was set in place. The totally unforeseen result was that files started to move around at high speed bearing little notes saying 'Fred, is this yours?' followed by 'No, try Charley' and so forth. Under this system Brownie points came easy.

FILES STARTED TO MOVE AROUND AT HIGH SPEED

10

A Rude Interruption

But, barely had I settled down to a life of regular hours
(those in private office were most decidedly *not*
regular) than the Suez crisis burst over our bewildered
heads. 'Gosh chaps, a war against the wogs! Should be easy.'
The trouble was that our gallant leaders had not foreseen
either the economic damage of the closure of the Suez Canal
or the loneliness of an alliance that included neither the
United States of America nor the Soviet Union. In short,
both France and we looked for trouble and found it.

The result in very short order was that we found ourselves
having to ration petrol and the chore of doing so rested on
the dear old Ministry of Fuel and Power. Coupons printed
years before were dug out from the cellar, local offices were
set up or converted and additional staff was hired. At the
same time enquiries poured in from the public and MPs and
a separate section was set up at HQ to handle them. And
guess whose recent experience won him the job of running
this section? Mine. Moreover, quite logically, my new section found itself responsible not only for answering letters
but also for dealing with the PQs and adjournment debates
that flourish when MPs are under pressure from their
constituents.

There was a lot of work about but again I enormously
enjoyed coping with it. So did my troops (a miscellaneous
bunch drawn from the highways and byways of Whitehall

and the local labour exchange) who backed me to the hilt. It is an interesting speculation whether our present government's apparent hatred of the motorcar will lead it down the logical road to rationing petrol again (I doubt it because, as the past four years have shown, the key difference between new and old Labour is the ability of the former to recognize a voter when it sees one.) But sometimes doctrine flourishes willy-nilly.

Nevertheless, should the need arise, whether through misplaced ideology or *force majeure*, I offer my successors three lessons from over forty years ago. The first is that people hoard coupons so you can safely issue more paper entitlements to petrol than you can honour. From memory we issued enough coupons in the first two or three months of the Suez crisis to sustain a higher level of consumption than had existed before the crisis began. Of course, the fact that we all knew the jig was up at a very early stage meant that we did not need to plan for a long haul. It really did help when our more importunate customers could be bought off with a few scraps of paper.

The second lesson was that a significant number of MPs (again from memory over half, spread pretty evenly between the parties) were actually the mindless pen pushers they professed to despise. The hallmark of these ladies and gentlemen was a printed slip whose wording ran something like:

Dear Minister,
　　I attach a letter dated —— from my constituent, Mr/Mrs —— of —— about petrol rationing. I would be grateful if you could let me have a reply, which I could pass on to Mr/Mrs ——.
　　Yours sincerely/fraternally,
　　(Joseph Soap MP for Llareggub)*

---

* With apologies to Dylan Thomas.

The great merit of this system was that a lazy or fence-sitting MP could leave it to his secretary/wife/mistress (or whoever was being paid by the rest of us to deal with his mail) to pick out the relevant incoming letters, fill out the covering slip and stick the lot in his (free) mail bag. In due course, a reply would come from the minister which could then be passed on to his constituent with a very short personal note adapted to reflect the nature of the reply ('the minister is too thick to understand your very cogent arguments' or, 'I'm brilliant. The minister gave in.')

Other MPs actually carried on a genuine dialogue with their constituents and tried to reason with them and explain the need for the rationing system as a means of sharing scarce resources fairly. These last served their country. The others served themselves.

The third lesson was that very few of our citizens thought lying to officialdom was in any way reprehensible. The rationing system naturally allowed for compassionate cases (notably the old and the sick) to be given extra coupons. In the early days of the scheme we were made aware of large numbers of one-legged grannies who drove 100 miles to church twice each Sunday and needed extra petrol to fuel their devotions. The trouble was that there were many genuine claims among the dross and a busy clerk had no reliable means of telling which were which. As failure would unleash the tabloids down the minister's throat and we had no KGB or Gestapo to pry into private lives, far too many liars were getting away with it. The solution came from a meeting the minister had with Lady Reading, the then head of that admirable body of dedicated ladies, the WVS (now the WRVS). They had performed admirable work during the war when they had tackled a wide variety of compassionate tasks such as feeding the fire fighters and other ARP services during the blitz and much, much more besides. In a sense, they were a vast new Salvation Army without the bands or the banners. Lady Reading offered their help in the present emergency and somehow the idea was born that we could use their existing network of committees and helpers to vet the compassionate claims for supplementary coupons. We therefore instructed our officials to refer all such claims to the local WVS. If they endorsed a claim we would accept it without further ado.

The system worked like a charm. It was one thing to lie to a faceless bureaucrat and quite another to lie to your neighbours. In putting the arrangements in place I could not help grinning at the memory of one of the earliest French films I had seen during the war — Fernandel in *Le Rosier de Madame Husson*. The plot here turns around an old lady, who, disgusted by the morals of her neighbours, leaves a prize to be awarded each spring to the most deserving virgin in the village. The mayor heads a committee of local worthies charged with selecting the prizewinner. As each candidate is introduced by her adoring *maman*, the committee dissolves into hoots of laughter. I hope the WVS found its task equally enjoyable.

Before the game was up my section answered thousands of letters (unfortunately we did not have time to count them), many hundreds of parliamentary questions and fielded a largish number of adjournment debates in both Houses. In career terms I began a long association with Parliament, which, besides being interesting, also chimed with a thread in my education (constitutional history in the sixth form and again at LSE) and my personal fascination with the histories of the English, French and American revolutions and their constitutional consequences.

All of this and my later experience in No 10 and the Cabinet Office have left me with a very keen interest in the reforms of our constitution now under active discussion and implementation. I will return to the central issues in this controversial field later in this book.

11

Again the Numbers Game

As the post-Suez dust settled on the ruins of defeated hopes and a discredited prime minister, it was back to stats and the numbers game. Leaving aside our senior management the key members of our statistical staff were the four statisticians — three proper ones and myself. The three were named Peter (a popular name in the 1920s), George and Tony. My namesake was a delightful genius whose basic qualifications were mathematical. He had the ability, and used it, to visualize the log and antilog tables and do quite complicated arithmetic in his head. He also had an oddball sense of humour. For example, he had two desks in his office at one of which he worked. The other was piled high with paper and files in a distinctly untidy heap. This was, he claimed, one of only two perfect filing systems. One was to give every piece of paper a separate file and to maintain a good index to them all. The drawback was that this system required a lot of work to keep it up to date and involved spending a lot of money on supporting staff. The alternative, which he used, was to keep all the paper in one place so that he always knew where each document was — on the other desk in front of him.

Peter, like me, was ex-navy and his experiences taught us all a lot. He had joined in the middle of the war and, when the navy found out that he could count, was trained as a radio mechanic in the Fleet Air Arm. This meant that he spent many months at school learning to trace breaks in the circuitry of British aircraft radios and repairing them with a soldering iron. Eventually, he passed his tests, was given the appropriate badges and was sent to join the new crew of a new American-built light fleet carrier allocated to the UK under lend-lease. Off they all went to the US of A to pick up their new charge. On arrival the Americans entertained them royally and allocated a number of senior naval technicians to show them the ropes in an unfamiliar vessel full of unfamiliar hardware including US aircraft.

So, on a wet and windy morning Peter and his friends found themselves on the flight deck of the carrier in the Norfolk navy yard. An American chief petty officer gathered them around a fighter plane and began his lesson.

Your job is to make sure that the pilot of this thing can keep in touch with his flattop at all times. The radio is behind this panel. If it doesn't work the first thing you do is to remove these screws and take off the panel, which you put on one side for reuse. You then undo the wires and nuts that connect the radio to the aircraft. A sharp pull and it comes away from the airframe. The next manoeuvre is to walk smartly to the side of the flight deck carrying the old radio, which you then throw overboard. Return to the aircraft, take a new radio out of its cardboard box and put it in the hole. Do up the internal wires and nuts. Replace the cover and do up its nuts. Job done.

Bang went six months' hard labour with the (now redundant) soldering iron.

For the record, Peter and his carrier then served with distinction in that hardest of all duties — the winter convoys to northern Russia.

As to George, and apart from his French wife (an acquisition I duplicated some years later), two things are of particular note. The first was that when last seen George was half way through reading (in French) the 13 volumes of *A la recherche du temps perdu* by Marcel Proust. The second was that, as a signalman, he had served with the Fourteenth Army in the final push of the war in Burma and had then gone on to help liberate Indonesia. His main memories of the Burma campaign were of sitting through interminable Indian films with his comrades in the twenty-sixth division of the Indian Army. And of Indonesia of fighting *with* the Japanese against the Indonesians rebelling against Dutch rule. Come on! I told you earlier that we were a crazy mixed-up generation.

Finally Tony, whose claim to fame was as a notable hockey player married to a member of a prestigious English women's hockey team. Tony finally shattered our visions of sweet helpless femininity by telling us of the slaughter that ensued when he organized a friendly game to be played between the ladies and his male team. The ladies allegedly won by three broken bones to nil.

The main bread-and-butter work of the division was to produce a great mass of routine energy statistics covering the activities of the fuel industries and its consumers, but most of this work went on in the engine room where the NCOs of the civil service delivered the goods. Us superior people made forecasts, wrote briefs and speeches for ministers, prepared the answers to PQs, handled the international aspects of our work, attended and wrote papers for Whitehall committees, meshed into the Treasury's machinery for controlling the investment programmes of the nationalized industries and generally practised the black arts. It is indicative of our status that our trade union (which mainly embraced administrators) was grandly called the First Division Association. Needless to say, this name reflected a staffing structure that had been superseded many, many years before. There was, of course, no extant second or third division either — that would have been too simple.

WINNING BY THREE BROKEN BONES TO NIL

It was in the course of this duty that I made my first visit to the OECD in Paris. My task was to support one of our undersecretaries in a debate on the outlook for energy supplies. He was our permanent representative on the committee and was very good at wheeling and dealing. Unfortunately, he was less good at numbers — hence my presence. Three things happened worthy of note. On the flight out (takeoff about 8.00 a.m.) I travelled first class because I was travelling with an undersecretary who was (in those days but no longer) entitled to first (I was not). So there was yet more *dolce vita* — we had champagne for breakfast and a free, if small, bottle of perfume for the wife, girlfriend or whatever. I said 'no thank you' to the champagne (earning a look of sheer incomprehension from my undersecretary) but 'yes please' to the perfume. It came in handy for bribing the typists to do a double type of documents of which more than eight copies were needed — even hammering the keys would not give more from carbon paper.

The second event was being met at Orly (Charles de Gaulle airport had not been built then) by the Italian delegate to the committee who was an old friend of my boss. This splendid mafioso (whom I had better call Guiseppe) was one of a breed of Italian businessmen who, in those days, were often asked to act as temporary delegates for the Italian government at international gatherings. Guiseppe's claim to fill the Italian seat stemmed from his business activities as an importer/exporter of oil. Indeed, rumour had it that, as the allied armies charged up the beach at Salerno, they were met by Guiseppe shouting 'anyone want a thousand barrels of fuel oil?'

The third event occurred in a square near the OECD building where the fountain in the middle was surrounded by tramps. Closer inspection showed them to be cleaning the labels off plastic water bottles salvaged from dustbins; filling them with water from the fountain; and sticking on new labels in a credible imitation of the real thing. A passing policeman took absolutely no notice.*

With the return of peace, life in the statistics' division settled down to an underlying rhythm, which became familiar to me in future years. Year one — the fun of finding out what the job was all about; year two — the doddle of repeating year one; year three — boredom sets in.

Luckily, an antidote appeared. In 1957 when, through mutual friends, I met a vivacious young French lady on the last day of my summer holidays. The next two years saw a

---

* The ability of the French police not to notice inconvenient illegality — as for example when the Channel ports are blockaded nowadays by striking fishermen, lorry drivers, prostitutes or whoever — is not a new phenomenon. Decades ago a popular French music hall ditty had a policeman explaining that, while old ladies and small children were legitimate targets for police action, *'les assassins sont pas pour nous'*.

spectacular long range courtship, which got all mixed up with scuba diving with a bunch of very wild Frenchmen, including one named, believe it or not, 'Jesus', the return of General de Gaulle to power in France, the mayhem of '*Algérie française*', the OAS, climbing to the summit of Stromboli, coming back to sea level in the dark down the scree slope, sleeping on beaches and in the luggage racks of trains and altogether having a whale of a time. At the end of this period two things happened. I was offered and turned down for personal reasons, the post of assistant petroleum attaché at the embassy in Washington; and I got married.

Besides all its other attractions the latter process was made professionally interesting by the insight it gave me into the very soul of French bureaucracy. We chose to marry in France and the law in that country requires (or required at that time) that whatever religious ceremony was undertaken there had to be a civil ceremony to make the marriage lawful — and French civil ceremonies require an awful lot of paper. As an example, my wife had to obtain from the French police a certificate listing all her various crimes and misdemeanours since leaving the crib. We have lived in terror of this document ever since because its pristine purity should have been, but was not, broken by a reference to a scandalous young trainee nurse riding her bicycle without a light on returning home from her hospital night shift.

My situation was even worse. I was, for example, required to produce a *certificat de résidence* to prove that I officially existed. Protestations that the Anglo-Saxon wilderness knew not such instruments of civilization were met with incredulity and the French version of 'then you can't get married in France can you, mate'. Luckily, the bureaucracy of my home town (then Richmond, Surrey) rose splendidly to the occasion and manufactured for me a beautiful *certificat* absolutely smothered in rubber stamps, which the *mairie* of Strasbourg swallowed like lambs.

Three more hurdles rose before our eyes as the countdown

to W-Day continued. The classic came from the insistence of French law that a prospective bridegroom must be able to demonstrate that he can support his beloved financially. As a foreigner this meant that I had to obtain a valid work permit allowing me to ply my trade in France. But the French are not idiots. They could see that if they gave me a work permit I might seek to obtain actual employment in their fair land. And if I did so I might deprive some worthy *citoyen* of his birthright. But Inspector Clouseau is not without guile. Let us insist, he said, that this man who is already robbing France of one of its fairest jewels should sign a solemn declaration that he will never seek to make use of his work permit actually to obtain work. So off I went to the *préfecture* to get this little lot in order.

On entering the holy portals I was directed to the relevant room, knocked on the door and was bidden to enter. Inside was a counter and behind it was a very bored looking *fonctionnaire* who listened to the explanation of my presence in stony silence. When I had finished he pointed to the door, which stood open behind me, and gestured to the notice on it. 'Can you read that?' he said. 'Yes,' said I, thinking this was some form of test of my comprehension of the French language. 'Please do so, out loud,' he said. I complied. The text said, 'THIS OFFICE IS OPEN FROM 1000 HRS UNTIL 1200 HRS AND FROM 1400 HRS UNTIL 1600 HRS'. My interlocutor looked at me with triumph in his eyes. 'It is now one minute past four,' he said. 'Come back in the morning.'

As this is meant to be a work of edification and learning I must digress briefly to look at the underlying lessons my experience teaches us about the French bureaucratic machine. That French bureaucrats are generally bloody-minded is a widely accepted truth. The reasons for this are, however, less well known. My view is that the fundamental flaw in the French system is the heavy overemphasis placed on academic attainment or rather on the outward and visible signs of such attainment represented by the bits of paper handed out to mark success in examinations. In France the exams taken by the young delimit their career prospects. If you want to be a railway porter you need one piece of paper. But if you want to be a stationmaster you need a better piece of paper and without it, however good you are, you are stuck. No wonder they had a revolution; what a pity it did not succeed.

Whatever one may think of the academic attainments of the British at least we do not, or did not, waste the talents of our practical men and women. In my day it was understood that half the promotions to principal (grade seven) were reserved for high flyers and the other half for 'promotees' from the lower ranks (indeed, several civil servants who entered the service at the bottom retired from the very top). *On est* more *égal que vous, Jacques.*

✳ ✳ ✳

But we must now go back to our obstacle course. The third moment of truth in our search for old-fashioned respectability came when we both went to the *mairie* two days before the wedding to see if all was in order. The friendly soul we spoke to (there are still some left) confessed that it was not. In particular, it appeared that the *préfecture*'s dossier on the event had not arrived with the *mairie* as it should have done. 'It is possible,' said our friendly soul, 'that they are being deliberately obtuse when we enquire of them. They do that sometimes to spite us. If I were you I would go to the *préfecture* and ask to be allowed to bring the papers here yourselves.' So we did and all was well.

The great day dawned and we arrived at the front steps of the *mairie* to be admitted by the guardians of the republic. As it happens these were the very steps where General de Gaulle had stood immediately after the liberation. Moreover, it was here that the great man had shaken the hand of a 12-year-old schoolgirl named Suzanne Elisabeth Horny who has not washed the relevant hand since.

As to the ceremony it was great fun and very French. The deputy mayor in his red, white and blue sash of office presided with panache as he read out chunks of the *Code Napoléon*. I particularly relished the bureaucratic flavour of the injunction to my wife that she must follow me anywhere 'unless I should seek to lead her into physical or moral danger'. It's a hard life.

After a honeymoon in Guernsey and going back to work, Suzanne moved into my ground floor flat in Sheen. Our garden in the shape of Richmond Park stretched five miles from our back door to Kingston upon Thames. We felt very rich.

12

Twilight Zone

E arly in 1958 the old wartime Ministry of Supply was wound up and its parts were distributed around Whitehall. Much of it fitted easily enough into other departments but one bit was difficult to place. The iron and steel division covered an industry that hung uneasily between the public and private sectors (indeed it was a prime example of the very wasteful yo-yo tendency in British politics in the second half of the twentieth century). Nationalized in 1949, denationalized in 1953, nationalized again in 1967 and finally denationalized in the 1980s, it took a six-month strike in 1980 to hammer home the basic industrial truth, once expressed by the head of the Chrysler Motor Company, that his firm was in business to make money not motorcars. At the time of which I now write the industry was largely in private hands, but supervised by a public board (the Iron and Steel Board) and regarded as an industry of fundamental national importance and thus a special case.

In the event it was decided that the industry should be entrusted to the tender mercies of the Ministry of Power (as it was then known) because it knew about nationalized industries. (Incidentally, the ministry's name when translated into French caused a deal of merriment among our French colleagues. 'Ho! Ho!' they said when told that one came from the '*Ministère de Puissance*'.)

When the steel industry came to us some ex-Ministry of Supply staff came with it. But there were gaps and I was posted to fill one of them.

My previous experience of industry at the operating level was confined to the oil companies — the famous Seven Sisters — each of which had a multinational persona, a larger budget than many countries, and a very high level of expertise in their chosen fields. The nationalized fuel industries were different. Each of them was engaged in attempting to catch up on the ravages of years of neglect and war. In this endeavour they suffered in varying degrees from inadequate management, shortage of cash for investment, political control of both capital spending and prices and Neanderthal trade unions. Real industry had so far passed me by — hence the heading of this chapter.

Within the division my role, as a principal, was to assist my elders and betters in handling the government's relations with the board and industry (including the industry's collective mouthpiece — the British Iron and Steel Federation); with the European Coal and Steel Community (which had its own treaty and existed independently of the Atomic and Economic Communities with its base and headquarters in Luxembourg); with the iron and steel scrap industry; and with the Commonwealth so far as the operation of imperial preference was concerned. Although assisting in the wider scene my personal responsibilities were for major investment projects, for iron and steel scrap exports and for the operation of imperial preference.

During my time in the division the main investment issue was the financing and siting of the so-called 'fourth strip mill'. The facts were these. The motorcar manufacturers and the makers of white goods (like refrigerators) needed good quality steel sheets from which to stamp out their products. Others (the makers of tin cans for the food industry, for example) needed good quality tin plate for similar purposes. The economic production of both required modern facilities that could make a uniform product in a continuous roll of steel sheet; and modern electrolytic tinning facilities that could cover that sheet in a uniform (and economically thin) layer of tin. Modern plants to make these materials existed in the UK but their production fell way behind demand and the gap was filled by expensive foreign imports and the continued output of very old (and well named) 'hand' mills. The latter, dating back to the middle of the nineteenth century, produced products of varying quality and were wasteful of both steel and tin. (For example, some made tinplate by dipping a sheet of steel into a bath of molten tin and then hanging it out to dry.) They were, frankly, totally outclassed in quality and price by the modern plants and had no future.

Plans were already afoot to provide modern tinning plant but the siting of a new strip mill was a matter of great political controversy because of the employment implications of both building and operating it. After a good deal of work by the ISB the possible sites were narrowed down to three: Immingham in England, a site near Glasgow owned by Richard, Thomas & Baldwin and Llanwern in South Wales owned by the Steel Company of Wales. The decision was important enough to be a matter for the Cabinet and was informed by factual assessments produced for the purpose. Actual knowledge of the assessments was kept very close — at least from junior characters like me — and I can only speculate. But rumour had it that the pecking order of suitability was first England, second South Wales, and third Scotland.

If this speculation is correct it is the more surprising that the final outcome was to ignore Immingham and split the project half and half between Scotland and Wales. The decision to favour the Celtic fringes over England was in line with the simplistic regional politics of the day founded on the sub-optimal approach of bringing the work to the workers (rather than as in prewar days bringing the workers to the work as when part of the Scottish steel industry moved south to Corby in the English Midlands). The decision to split the mill in two was, however, plain daft. Rolling mills that made continuous steel sheet required to be fed by massive slabs of steel specially produced for the purpose. The plant used to make these slabs had a minimum size sufficient to serve a full-scale rolling mill. Splitting the mill meant having two half used slabbing facilities where one would have sufficed and two rolling mills instead of one with all the attendant costs of duplication. Not for the first time (and not the last) political needs overthrew industrial good sense — or so it seemed to this independent observer. It was, of course, also the case that given the usual games of musical chairs played by governments, ministers and officials, those who took the decisions had moved on before the chickens could come home to roost.

It should be noted in passing that while the speed of rotation of officials has been somewhat slowed down in recent years, ministers still move from job to job at a dizzying rate. Moreover, the training of officials has been massively improved in the 30 years since the Fulton Report (of which more in due course) so that ministers, and the MPs from whom most are recruited, remain the only 'enthusiastic amateurs' left in government. The result is that only the best of them really know what they are doing and virtually none are held personally accountable for their actions. Add to this that, within the European Union at any rate, they have to do battle with, say, French ministers many of whom are highly trained professional civil servants (ministers and officials are interchangeable in France) with several years of intense postgraduate training in all aspects of their trade (including the skills of negotiation) and the cost of our neglect becomes apparent.

Before leaving the story of the strip mills I should also say a bit more about the obverse of the medal — the closure of the old hand mills. As already mentioned they had no future so that the people they employed had to find other work.

The consequence was a steady flow of deputations to see the minister, almost always accompanied by their local MP and quite often by Jim Griffith, the highly respected elder states-man of the Labour Party in Wales. These were always sad occasions because the delegates were transparently honest and bewildered men and the comfort we could give was usually very limited. Moreover, local history and culture added to the pain. We urban characters were totally con-ditioned to travelling twenty miles or so each day and each way to and from work and to moving house, on average, every seven years or so — often to other parts of the country or even abroad. They, on the other hand, seemed to regard visiting the next valley as an adventure and moving house (at all, let alone to the next valley) as a domestic disaster. Coming to terms with the reality that, even if we succeeded in bringing new work to Wales (which we did), their lives would never be the same again was for many of them the hardest cross of all to bear.

However, every job has its light relief and in the iron and steel division mine was my work with the scrap merchants. I do not say that *Steptoe and Son* was based on reality but it had the same relationship to the spirit of the industry as *Yes Minister* has to Whitehall, or *Dad's Army* has to the Home Guard (I should know having been part of both). I particu-larly relished the annual dinner of the scrap merchants held in one of the posh hotels in Park Lane. After all I was a boy from the back streets of north London and could lapse into the vernacular at a second's notice (just as I could lapse into broad Mummerset learned during my teen years in rural Northamptonshire). But the real point at issue in my deal-ings with my clients was the availability of export licences for scrap. As I have already mentioned, the prices to be obtained for scrap metal abroad were markedly higher than at home where they were controlled. So export licences had a considerable cash value. Fortunately for me, no one in my tenure of office offered me a bribe. Perhaps they thought I was too pure (or too wet) to be vulnerable. Perhaps, too, I was shielded to some extent by my number two who was a veteran of war surplus sales in the Ministry of Supply and whose desk carried a notice giving the minimum bribe he would consider given the risks he would run to his pension. It was a lot of money.

Finally, there was imperial preference. This system, by which the anti-marketeers of the day set much store, was one that sought to turn the Commonwealth into a low, or zero, tariff area. The problem with it was that it was not even-handed in its favours and, as so often, its defenders lived in cloud cuckoo land. Thus, what the agreement actually said was that preferential tariffs would apply to imports from Britain into Commonwealth countries whenever we could show that we could provide equivalent supplies to those on offer from third countries. Think about it. In the case of Australia, for example, I used to receive a stream of telegrams saying, in effect, we have a cargo of Japanese steel three weeks out from Sydney harbour. If you can match the delivery time we will waive the duty. Big deal!

Incidentally, it was during this period that I became progressively more involved with the OECD of which we were founder members; and the EEC where we acquired a form of observer status as a preliminary to the possibility of membership. The OECD was a doddle because the organization had no real power and its meetings largely took the form of reports on what was going on at home coupled with rather academic discussions of the economic situation. The EEC, on the other hand, was bewildering. Every discussion here was larded with the opinions of the Commission's lawyers, which were delivered in a pompous manner, in a variety of foreign languages and through a fog of translation of dubious quality. The treaties were everything and were referred to as if they were Holy Writ. The reality was, of course, that they were a good deal more complex than, and vastly more obscure than, the Ten Commandments and thus superb lawyer fodder. Add to this real doubt about whether the legal jargon of the French and German basic texts (which had equal validity) actually said the same thing and your average British minister and official felt as uncomfortable as the fabled princess with a pea under her mattress.

This is the moment, I think, to give a touch of well-deserved immortality to my immediate boss — one Jimmy Wilson. Jimmy was a stocky man and a devout Catholic who had spent much of the war cooped up in besieged Malta firing anti-aircraft guns at the Luftwaffe and its Italian mates (if so prickly a relationship could be described as matey). Usually Jimmy and I split the chore of attending meetings in Brussels and travelled, necessarily, as singletons. On one occasion, however, we both went to Brussels on the same day to attend two different meetings and agreed to meet up for the return journey at the central station. I arrived there a little after Jimmy and was staggered to find him, dressed in his habitual bowler hat and pinstriped trousers, sitting on a bench and feeding a tiny infant from a bottle. On seeing my (very British) raised eyebrow, Jimmy explained that the mother had asked him to take over while she went urgently to the loo. I immediately feared the worst and envisioned a fleeing mother abandoning her infant and leaving us to explain ourselves to the usually bad tempered Flemish policemen who inhabited the station. Luckily, just at that moment the lady in question reappeared uttering copious thanks, and took the cooing infant away from his temporary daddy. Jimmy looked smug and muttered something about the value of a Catholic upbringing.

Before bringing this chapter to a close I must tell you about my then permanent secretary, Sir John Maude (later Lord Redcliffe-Maude). John was a brilliant academic who came into government service during the war and stayed on after it was over. He was intelligent, humane and very, very funny. Three moments remain firmly in my memory. First, there was the occasion when we lent a lot of money to

Richard, Thomas & Baldwin to help finance their steel investment programme. I had been involved in the negotiations and as the day came near for signing the loan agreement, was dispatched to find the ministry's official seal,

THE VALUE OF A CATHOLIC UPBRINGING

which would be needed to validate the document. This rarely used piece of kit was finally unearthed and proved to be a massive artefact of wriggly cast iron with a long handle protruding from the top. Pour in your hot wax; pull down said handle and, bingo, a beautiful medieval seal several inches in diameter. As the great day dawned John invited me, as the youngest member of the team, to come and pull the handle. And when the job was done he invited me to stay on for a whisky 'to help you recover from your heavy physical exertions'.

The second treasured moment came when, at some function in the ministry, he told us the story of a game favoured in his university days that involved dreaming up new collective nouns. He said that his favourite was a collective noun for a group of harlots — 'a flourish of strumpets'.

The third came at his retirement from the department when he went off to become the UK's high commissioner in South Africa. His speech of farewell touched at one point on the lessons he was undertaking to give him a grounding in the Afrikaans language. He had been astonished, he said, to learn that if he took his car to have its back axle greased the words to use were '*smeer my as*'. He was sorely missed.

✻ ✻ ✻

Our first son John was born in Kingston upon Thames in April 1960. Our second son Oliver was born in Richmond-upon-Thames in June 1961. We moved to a semidetached house in Twickenham in 1962. Our next-door neighbour, a widow of indeterminate age, always wore a hat. She is known in the family's collective memory as '*la dame au chapeau vert*'.

13

Into the Lion's Den

And then, frabjous day, the UK actually applied for membership of the three communities. Negotiations began early in Brussels (for the Common Market proper) and in Paris for Euratom. Negotiations in Luxembourg for the Coal and Steel Community were delayed and did not begin until June 1962. The arrangement for handling the negotiations in Luxembourg followed those already in place in Brussels and Paris. A small team of FCO and home department officials was established in each city where the negotiations were to take place and a further corps of officials were established in London who handled coordination at home and came out to take part in the actual negotiations as circumstances required. The leadership of the Luxembourg team was given to a Ministry of Power undersecretary and I was appointed as the Ministry of Power's anchor man in Luxembourg. My heavily pregnant wife and I packed our children and other belongings into our old Vauxhall estate car (bench seat in the front, gear change on the steering column, rust everywhere) and set out for foreign parts. Near the end of our journey the kids, who had been very resilient to that point, began to show signs of having had enough of the Ardennes and we looked around for somewhere to stay the night. We found it in a small village where the lady who owned the hotel looked at our children with distaste but finally took us on as avarice overcame caution. The only other point of note is that, as my wife (who is, dare I say it, a fresh air fanatic) pulled back the curtains of our bedroom, Madame, the proprietress, shrieked with pain and shouted, 'No, no, nòt wiz ze fingers, pull ze string.'

Next day we arrived in Luxembourg and established ourselves in a rented house near the Arbed steel works (everything in Luxembourg city was near the Arbed steel works) and got ready to negotiate/give birth as our share of family duties required.

Thereafter things moved fast. We explored Luxembourg and got our bearings; I moved into our new office near the centre of town, linked up with the rest of the team and Suzanne and I went shopping. This is where Suzanne made her mark on the local inhabitants. The point is that Suzanne, for historical reasons, is fluent in three languages — French, German and Alsatian (which is a local dialect halfway between Swiss German and the dialect of Lorraine/Luxembourg). In we went to our local food store to order food for four and a half hungry mouths. A little group of local ladies was in the shop gossiping with the proprietor — in French. So Suzanne, to be friendly, also spoke to the shopkeeper in French. To our astonishment the locals promptly switched to German and quick-witted Suzanne did the same. Shock, horror! The locals then made a further switch to *Letzeburgisch*. Undaunted, Suzanne switched to Alsatian and the ladies fled defeated, muttering (in assorted languages), 'you can't have a private chat anywhere nowadays.'

A few days later and the great man himself — Edward Heath, Lord Privy Seal — arrived for the opening meeting. There was lots of hot air in the morning as the platitudes flew and then the Prime Minister of Luxembourg invited all present to lunch. We left the conference hall in a fleet of cars and set off for an unknown destination. Half an hour later we were still *en route* and doubts began to creep into our minds. Were we about to fall over the edge into France, Belgium or Germany? But then we stopped in a fairytale setting and entered a large restaurant. When we were all seated I remarked to my Luxembourg neighbour that, while the restaurant and its surroundings were attractive, I had not expected to travel quite so far to find it. His reply began the insidious process of undermining my puritan naïvety. 'Oh', he said, 'this restaurant is owned by the minister of X's aunty and it is her turn.'

It says something for my mental processes that, while I cannot remember what we ate, I have a very clear memory of Ted Heath's bad joke. I am sure it was actually an old one but it came fresh to me. 'My Lords, Prime Minister, Ministers, Ladies and Gentlemen,' he began, 'some of you may be wondering about the strange ministerial title I bear. It would take a lengthy history lesson to explain it fully but I can assure you that I am neither a lord, a privy nor a seal.' The ensuing silence of non-comprehension was broken only by some half suppressed sniggers from the Brits present.

This episode came to mind again some time later when the FCO produced a very useful little guidebook for British officials attending meetings of Community members. Among lots of good advice it counselled avoiding shaggy dog stories like the plague. It went on to say that if anyone tried this heavily Anglo-Saxon genre of humour a listener to the simultaneous translation would be likely to hear 'the British delegate is now telling a story that is quite untranslatable, but it would be polite if you could laugh — *now.*'

Thereafter the negotiating machine rolled forward and it rapidly became apparent that the French would do their (very competent) utmost to delay and, if possible, wreck the whole business. The General wanted his revenge for wartime slights, real or imagined, and the Germans, carrying their load of guilt around with them, looked on like hypnotized rabbits. It is one of the ironies of the age that the Germans and French have since totally reversed their 1960s' roles of mistress and poodle.

As negotiators we faced four hurdles. The active hostility of the French (as a disciplined force and not as individuals. Indeed many of their officials disliked the line they were required to follow — though most enjoyed the high-class game of chess that resulted from it); the neutrality of the Germans; the weakness of the remaining four; and the success of the French in persuading all the other members of the 'six' that they had to agree to a single line on any issue before discussing it with us. This latter point meant that many of the real negotiations happened within the six where we could only be present by proxy.

As an illustration of what this meant there was an occasion when we had spent a great deal of time briefing the delegate of one of the smaller countries on a particular issue. When the relevant meeting of the six had finished we asked him how he had got on. 'Badly,' he said in all seriousness. 'You see I came halfway down the pass list of the École Nationale d'Administration (which accepts a leavening of foreign students) and the French leader came top. I didn't stand a chance.' (We understood what he meant because the Frenchman concerned was held in awe by his compatriots as the only French civil servant who had ever worked voluntarily on Christmas day.)

An unusual example of a one-off negotiating hurdle occurred towards the end of 1962. The interpreters we were expecting for a meeting of the seven (namely a joint meeting of both sides) got lost in a snowdrift (or a pub) somewhere between Strasbourg and Luxembourg. 'Goody,' said the French, 'let's go home until after Christmas.' 'Nonsense,' we said, 'who needs interpreters? We can cope.' Surprisingly, the French agreed, perhaps out of curiosity, and the meeting got underway. The French stuck to the French language. The Germans, whose English was much better than their French, tried desperately to say as little as possible. The Italians just

looked confused and used whatever language came to hand
— pidgin franglais someone described it as. And the Benelux
countries used English as if they had invented it. We mainly
spoke French although our gallant leader launched into German from time to time. And therein lay the problem. Our
leader had learned his German during a year spent before
the war at a German university studying something else. The
language he learned then was, it turned out, akin to the
English my father and his friends had taught their guards at
a prisoner of war camp in the First World War. 'Ripe' in the
language of the time.

Thus, when my boss told the German's boss gently that he
was mistaken about something, we were all surprised when
the German turned bright red and stalked out of the room.
It took two weeks of intense diplomatic activity to get him
back in again.

The loss of the interpreters was an example of the fun and
games introduced into our lives by the relative isolation of
the grand duchy. In the winter months, at any rate, travel by
road and/or rail was uncertain and time consuming. It may
seem odd to say that travel by air was the preferred route,
but it had one great advantage. NATO had built up Luxembourg's airport to be big enough to accommodate fully laden
B-52s. It was (and still is) what the young nowadays call
'ginormous'. This description applies, of course, to the
runways and meant that civilian planes had a good margin
for error when they came in to land. The terminal building
remained a small wooden hut.

The real disadvantage of the airport was its vulnerability
in winter to snow, ice and fog. The latter could be a nuisance. Snow and ice, however, brought out the full ingenuity
of the (part-time) airport manager. His technique was to
drive his Jeep onto the runway, career down it until he
reached a preset speed, slam on the brakes and measure the
skid marks. If they were longer than X metres he declared
the airport shut and went home.

The amount of traffic using the airport was small and mainly consisted of battered aircraft bearing company names that were not of the household variety. Most of them operated charter flights apparently designed to circumvent the state-backed cartels that kept the airfares of the day at ludicrous heights. For some reason many of them seemed to be flying to Reykjavik. Scheduled flights were few and far between but included the aged war-surplus Dakotas operated by LuxAir, which mostly plied to and from Brussels but occasionally took in Paris and one or two other places as well. At this time there were no direct flights to London and most travellers took BEA (as it then was) or Sabena for the London/Brussels leg of the journey. This part of the journey was flown in Caravelles, Vikings and Viscounts and similar long forgotten but sturdy aeroplanes. By contrast, the second leg of the journey in second-hand war-surplus Dakotas was an *adventure* – very primitive but great fun for those, like the members of my family, who were not, as they say, of a nervous disposition.

It is worth recording, if only to illustrate the spirit of the age, that on one trip from Luxembourg to Paris by LuxAir the plane was overbooked and had a surplus passenger. The problem was solved, not by a heated argument ending in expulsion, but by the stewardess giving her seat to the surplus body and sitting on the floor.

Local transport presented a different problem. Walking was OK in Luxembourg city in what were then relatively uncrowded streets. Indeed, the only problem with walking came from the highly over disciplined Luxembourg pedestrians who obeyed the traffic signs even when there was no traffic. Oh the delays! Do anthropomorphic motorcars, I ask myself, feel frustration in the same way and for the same reasons?

In 1962 Luxembourg's bicycles and mopeds, like those of the rest of continental Europe, came out in droves four times a day. To work in the morning; back home for lunch; back

78

to work two hours' later; and back home again in the evening. To sit in a motorcar and see the advancing hordes of bikes and mopeds was to experience a little of the feeling of the royalist infantry when they saw Oliver Cromwell and his Ironsides charging down on them at Marston Moor.

Of course, there were buses but they were crowded, smelly and uncertain. They were also far below the dignity of the politicians and functionaries of the Commission and the diplomatic corps, even from the most democratic of continental countries. This stricture does not apply to the Brits who normally will accept anything in the way of discomfort without noticing it. In our case, I am convinced that the problem was simply a failure to understand how to buy a ticket.

But the real fact of local travel was that the motorcar was king. And if one had a chauffeur as well 'Yippee!' The truly prestigious motorcars were Mercs or Citröen DSs. But we Brits got one up by sheer eccentricity. We not only had a sit-up-and-beg Austin Princess of enormous dimensions; we also had a green goddess to drive it. For the uninitiated a green goddess was a chauffeuse from the government car pool who wore a green uniform and was another wartime hangover on a par with the Cabinet Office mess. Needless to say, both our car and its driver attracted a good deal of attention. And never more so than on the day when it broke down in the snow. Imagine the scene — large car stationary in the snow disgorging a seemingly endless flow of Brits from its interior. The assembled UK delegation then puts its collective shoulder to the wheel and pushes Mr Austin's heavy product through the snow to the nearest garage.

Other highlights for me included the time our boss came back from a late night meeting with his French counterpart with acute food poisoning. All he could tell me was that the meeting had gone as expected and that London was very anxious to know how he had got on. Could I try and cope? Thereupon, and full of the brashness of youth, I drafted, and sent to London, a reporting telegram about a meeting of which I knew very little but which I constructed by following closely the known party line of both sides. And in the morning my boss, slightly recovered, endorsed it as accurate.

Another was the occasion when fog stopped the London party reaching us for a meeting and only Ian Byatt, a Treasury economist (later of Ofwat fame) who came on from a meeting in Brussels, made it to Luxembourg. Again there were signs of jubilation in the French delegation (they must have had bonuses for avoiding meetings with us) but Ian and I decided that we knew enough about the British national insurance system to fight off French charges of unfairness. So we fought, bluffed and survived.

On the social side the highlight of the whole experience was when the Grand Duchess took the occasion of her birthday to invite the entire diplomatic corps to go with her to the cinema. The film was *The Longest Day* and, to my lasting regret, I was unable to study the faces of my European colleagues when the lights went down.

In the middle of all this my beloved wife gave birth to our third son, Philip, who thereby enjoyed the benefits of Luxembourg citizenship. The local pop group of the time consisted of a bunch of singing nuns (Les Soeurs Sourire) who were out to show the youngsters that, despite appearances, the Catholic Church was 'with it'. As Suzanne had Philip in a Catholic clinic, and the new record (disc) was very popular, she came out knowing all the words by heart.

And then the General, knowing that, once again, the Anglo-Saxons were slowly but surely winning, pulled the plug. It was an incredibly emotional time. Belgians cursed, Dutchmen wept, Frenchmen looked uncomfortable (which for *Enarques* is quite something), Italians shrugged their shoulders and Germans tried hard not to say 'so we have won after all'.

As for us we remained phlegmatic to the end. One small triumph was to keep a current meeting of the seven going beyond the announcement of the General's veto (which seemed important at the time). Otherwise, it was a round of farewell parties followed by taking the family home by air and then going back to pick up our car and residual belongings. When I drove home through the Ardennes they were still covered in snow and looked much as they must have done in the winter of 1944/5. Bastogne seemed particularly ghostly with the memorial of the siege (a battered Sherman tank) standing out starkly from the wintry scene. Once again I asked the wind the unanswered question, 'Did the American General MacAuliffe really answer "nuts" when called upon to surrender Bastogne or did he use a more soldierly expression?' As reported, the incident just does not ring true unless the word means different things either side of the Atlantic (answers on a postcard please — regret no prizes).

14

A Scientific Interlude

On return from Luxembourg I found myself (perhaps as a reward for hard work but perhaps only as a penalty for allegedly soft living) whisked off to our scientific division. This, besides being responsible for the safety in mines research establishment, disposed of funds for research elsewhere, kept a close eye on the research activities of our nationalized industries (the minister had to approve their programmes) and managed a major scientific advisory committee, which concerned itself among other things with energy conservation. Most of the staff were scientists but they had one administrator (me) to act as lead secretary to their advisory and other committees; to take charge of (and be responsible for) their money; to supervise their expenditure and make sure it stayed within the rules; and crucially to deal with the Treasury on financial matters including the annual operating budget.

I was not left in this job for long and so did not go as far as I would have liked in absorbing the ethos of our scientific community. Nevertheless, I learned some useful lessons. I came in contact with the ins and outs of financial control; I saw the immense patience needed to conduct some scientific experiments; I found out that senior scientists lived much higher on the hog than I had realized; and I learned the nature of a 'Barnsley chop'.

The experiment that impressed me most was neither

expensive nor costly. A lot of explosive is used in mining coal and setting off one deliberate explosion can sometimes cause unwanted, and indeed dangerous, secondary ones. The experiment sought to find out how the firing of one piece of mining explosive caused the unintentional explosion of another piece of such explosive in reasonable proximity to the first. Was the medium a shock wave, as some believed, or the passage of a physical particle from one piece of explosive to the other? The researcher involved sought to uncover the truth and to this end tried to photograph the primary and secondary explosions simultaneously. When last seen by me he was trying to build a super fast camera for the purpose and hoped to arrive at exposures of one-millionth of a second only. We all wished him luck in his endeavour.

The scientific 'boys' also had fun in a spectacular experiment whose purpose I cannot now remember but which consisted of letting two wagons laden with coal collide with each other at very high speed. Just think, they actually got paid for enjoying themselves. We pen pushers came away from these games absolutely convinced that we had chosen wrongly in setting out on our careers — silly billies as Denis Healey would undoubtedly have characterized us had he been asked.

As to a Barnsley chop, this consisted of some six or seven ordinary lamb chops held together as nature intended and providing a man-sized meal for a 16-stone navvy. (For the uninitiated a 'navvy' was originally a skilled labourer who dug canals, which in the eighteenth century were known as navigations. Confusing isn't it?)

I was just getting my feet comfortably under the scientific table when the call came out of the blue at the beginning of 1963. 'Off you go to join the Cabinet secretariat. It will be for a two-year stint.' As it happened, the immediate stint in Cabinet Office and No 10 was to extend to about five years and my eventual career service in Cabinet Office in its various guises and including No 10, totalled about twelve years. Maurice Hankey (the first Cabinet secretary) and I will have a lot to talk about should we chance to meet in the next world.

A SPECTACULAR EXPERIMENT

15

Number 70 Whitehall

Before launching into an account of my life in the Cabinet secretariat I must give you, gentle reader, a brief account of what the Cabinet Office is and what it does. This is necessary, not only because there is no non-specialist textbook or literature about the Cabinet Office as a whole (which is generally unknown to the public at large beyond some passing references in Len Deighton's spy novels) but because, amoeba like, it changes its shape and responsibilities from one administration to the next.

What is the Cabinet Office?

The key point is that the Cabinet Office is actually two distinct organisms that only come together in the person of the secretary of the Cabinet and through some shared common services like the provision of accommodation, messengers and so on. These are the Cabinet secretariat proper, invented and constructed in 1916 by the then prime minister Mr David Lloyd George; and the Cabinet Office as a piece of administrative machinery that can only be described as a ragbag into which each administration pours those centralized functions the prime minister of the day wants to keep under his or her eye. Most of these like, for example, the recruitment and training of the civil service can be centralized, decentralized, added to, subtracted from or split up according to the fashions of the moment. However, underlying the history of the central departments are two hidden agendas.

The first, which varies from prime minister to prime minister, is the extent to which the incumbent wishes (or is able) to be a forceful leader on the lines of an American president or is content to be a chairman or chairwoman in the Attlee mould. The second is a real power struggle between the Cabinet Office (in its ragbag guise) and the Treasury for control of the commanding heights of Whitehall, for example, through the provision of advice to the PM on the machinery of government issues. This is a struggle in which the emergence and subsequent demise of the civil service department was only a passing aberration of the corporate state. My personal belief is that something like the present compromise will endure if only for the pragmatic and mundane reason that putting everything, apart from the secretariat, back in the Treasury (as it was 50 years ago) would overload Treasury ministers to the point of managerial lunacy; and creating an overt prime minister's department would do much the same for the prime minister.

Cabinet Office: Where is it?

Thus 'back to our sheep' as our French neighbours so curiously put it when they mean 'back to the main issue'. Let us begin at the front door. The entrance to the modern Cabinet Office lies in the middle of the façade of the so-called 'Old Treasury' building in Whitehall opposite Richmond Terrace. This building, dating from the early eighteenth century and known to the postman as No 70 Whitehall is, in fact, part of a complex of seventeenth and eighteenth century buildings running from the park end of Downing Street along the north side of that road, round the corner into Whitehall and then north again to the much photographed entrance to Horse Guards Parade. The Old Treasury, like much of Whitehall, is built on the site of the old Palace of Whitehall and actually incorporates parts of that palace (including the foundation of a Tudor cockpit and a splendid Tudor window) in its fabric. These relics survive because the eighteenth century builder was a frugal man who did not waste good brickwork if it could be incorporated in the structure replacing it. All of these buildings are internally connected (there are lots of backdoors to No 10) and among the interconnections is the famous 'green baize door' separating the secretariat's offices from No 10.

The whole area, of course, abounds in history. One little known example, which appeals to me as a Civil War buff, is that the mounted soldiers guarding the Whitehall gate to the Horse Guards Parade belong to a regiment (now known as the Household Cavalry Regiment), which is a direct descendant of both Prince Rupert's cavalry and Oliver Cromwell's Ironsides. Moreover, both these 'bodies of horse' were present at the decisive Civil War battle that took place on the afternoon of 14 June 1645 at Naseby in Northamptonshire and that set all on course for the revolutionary settlement of 1688 and ultimately for today's constitutional arrangements. To walk in that building is to feel the past.

Cabinet Office: Origins of the Secretariat

So much for the setting, now let us look at the origins. Cabinet government in the UK evolved gradually over the years spanning the period between the Civil War when Parliament ran both the country and the war by committee, to the present day with 'New' Labour apparently playing a frenetic game of blind man's bluff with the constitution. Intermediate constitutional milestones were the Glorious Revolution of 1688; the advent of the Hanoverians (more or less on contract) when George I, speaking no English, left running the government to Robert Walpole (who thereby became our first prime minister and the one, moreover, who consolidated the dominance of the Cabinet through his masterly use of the patronage attaching to his office); the great Reform Acts of the nineteenth century; and the Parliament Act of 1912. The really astonishing feature of this part of our history, however, is that, throughout two turbulent centuries (which embraced events of the magnitude of the American and French revolutions externally and the Industrial Revolution at home) and thereafter through until the First World War the British Cabinet functioned without a secretariat and no records of its meetings were kept beyond the private notes of the ministers present and the weekly report made by the prime minister to the sovereign of the day. As government became more and more complicated the disadvantages of the lack of records and of accurate instructions to departments became apparent. The Boer War led to the provision of a specialized secretariat to support the ministerial committee on defence and, when David Lloyd George became prime minister late in 1916 one of his first acts was to create a secretariat for the Cabinet proper. His reasoning and the action he took were well described in his wartime memoirs. The relevant extract from these (vol. 1, p. 643) reads:

Cabinet Office: Lloyd George's Memoirs

Another departure from Cabinet traditions which I had decided to initiate was the setting up of a Cabinet Secretariat. Hitherto no written record was ever made of even the most important decisions of the Cabinet, let alone the discussions which preceded them. I have no recollection of Sir Henry Campbell Bannerman or Mr Asquith ever making a note of the decisions arrived at, except in very exceptional cases where the decision was to be embodied in the form of an answer to a question about to be put in the House of Commons. The result was that now and again there was a good deal of doubt as to what the Cabinet had actually determined on some particular issue. I came to the conclusion that it was desirable to have a secretary present who would make a short précis of the discussions on all important issues and take a full record of all decisions. Where these decisions affected one of the Departments, a copy of the Minute was immediately sent to the Minister concerned. I thought it was of primary importance that a written intimation of the character and terms of the decision of the Cabinet should be sent formally to the Department, not merely as a reminder to the Minister, but in order that the officials who advised him and carried out his orders should be fully informed. I also thought it not only desirable but imperative, having regard to the number of decisions taken in the past which had not been carried out, to charge the Secretary with the duty of keeping in touch with further developments. And reporting to me from time to time what action had been taken in the various Departments concerned on these Cabinet orders. I subsequently found that these enquiries addressed from the Cabinet Office, and the reports which had to be made in response, were very helpful in keeping the departments alert and well up to the mark. Where the Secretary reported failure or delay in carrying out decisions, I sent for the Minister, and where unexpected difficulties had arisen, steps were taken to remove them.

The first Secretary appointed to this responsible and confidential position was Sir Maurice Hankey. He discharged his very delicate and difficult function with such care, tact and fairness that I cannot recall any dispute ever arising as to the accuracy of his minutes or his reports of the action taken.

Despite an attempt by Mr Bonar Law in the early 1920s to

get rid of it, the secretariat has continued virtually unchanged to this day.

Cabinet Office: Ethos

The Cabinet secretariat has a total staff of getting on for one hundred people, of whom about a dozen are high flying, young or youngish, committee secretaries and the rest are support staff ranging from clerks and typists to messengers and guards. The support staffs are, for the most part, permanent employees of the Cabinet Office as a whole. The committee secretaries are all, with the exception of the Cabinet secretary himself, drawn on short-term secondments (usually for two or three years) from line departments. This outsourcing of the key talents required for the job fulfils several objectives. It gives the office a steady flow of fresh minds; it provides the office with up-to-date expertise; it greatly inhibits the development of separate Cabinet Office policies; and it provides the office, over time, with a network of contacts at the higher levels in departments who understand its needs and can respond intelligently and quickly to requests for help.

The arrangements described above for staffing the office are, I believe, of cardinal importance for its undoubted success. The point is that the Cabinet secretariat is not a policy forming, but a policy facilitating, organism. It provides a forum and framework within which ministers can formulate policy in an orderly and informed manner. But to do this successfully and speedily it needs to enjoy the unstinted trust of ministers in its fairness and of departmental officials in its competence. It has earned that trust in the past. Long may this happy state continue!

* * *

On looking back at this chapter it seems a bit solemn. So let us bring it to an end with a little doggerel written by some anonymous Cabinet Office scribe years ago and preserved in the archives ever since. Thus:

And so, as the great ones go home to their dinner,
The Secretary sits getting thinner and thinner,
As he cudgels his brains to record and report,
What he thinks,
That they'll think,
That they ought to have thought!'

* * *

At this time we moved to a new house on a new estate on the south bank of the Thames above Hampton Court. Our neighbours were all, what would later be known as 'yuppies'. Everyone, including the children, lived in each other's houses and had a whale of a time within the constraints of fairly modest incomes. The spirit of the place was well captured when, one Sunday, our youngest son fell over and badly bit his tongue. Our neighbour, an up and coming surgeon ('I am the world's greatest expert on two inches of the human gut') rushed him in his car to a famous London teaching hospital, caused an operating theatre to be opened up, and stitched the tongue back on, just like that.

16

Back to the Learning Curve

When I arrived at the secretariat at the beginning of 1963 the last possible date for the next election (1964) was rapidly approaching. The Tories would, by then, have been in power for 13 years and Harold Wilson was already honing the slogan of the '13 wasted years of Tory misrule'. The feeling I had was that the government saw disaster staring it in the face and while Alec Douglas Home was both bright and good he was too much of a gentleman for the really dirty work of political infighting. Moreover, as seen from the secretariat, the Tory government was both tired and devoid of new ideas. Pressure groups gathered around the sickbed and, as Whitehall wags put it, the result appeared too often to be (in the words of a popular game show of the time) 'Give 'im the money Barney!' For many of us at or near the centre, as for many senior people in industry and commerce, the wish was not so much for a government of a different complexion as for one that had a coherent strategy and the will to carry it through. Our most fervent wish was for an end to dithering and Harold Wilson appeared to offer it. Of course the new Labour government that came to power a year later did not realize, at first, that most of us were apolitical. Too many of them committed the politicians' besetting sin of believing their own propaganda. And too many of them did not realize that the 'committed' civil servant is a dangerous

THE RT. HON. BARON WILSON OF REIVAULX KG FRS,
PRIME MINISTER 1964–70 AND 1974–76

animal to have around the house. As Oliver Cromwell said so long ago, 'the state in seeking men to serve it is not concerned with their opinions. So long as they are willing faithfully to serve, that satisfies.' That qualification is the vital one.

Five vignettes from that time will serve to illuminate the two governments spanning this period and divided by the general election of 1964. First, the result of many years of joint endeavour by the Conservative ministers of the day meant that they could, as colleagues do, talk shorthand to each other. Imagine the poor secretary of the committee where the discussion went as follows:

> *Chairman*: 'Here's a nice mess. What are we going to do about it?'
> *First Minister*: 'Surely we had a situation like this about a year ago? I remember that old Fred suggested — —.'
> *Second minister*: 'That's right. It worked too. Let's do it again.'
> *Chairman*: 'Good idea. Next item.'

Next, a committee discussing a proposal to put an overhead power cable in a sensitive national park and considering the cost (many millions of pounds) of putting it underground. Suddenly a minister breaks in with, 'Do we really have to accept that electricity pylons are ugly? Our Victorian ancestors would have been proud of them as symbols of progress and the French regard the Eiffel Tower as a major national monument.' It was a very refreshing, if politically incorrect, moment.

Third, came summer of 1963. These were still the days when gentlemen went off on 12 August to shoot little birds and the secretariat more or less packed up. Two of us were left in charge of the whole shebang. Me because, with very small children I was not tied to school holidays for my leave and Philip the number two in the office who was similarly not tied to August because his children had grown up. We both settled down to a routine of positively no meetings but lots of time to catch up with reading, or the latest exhibition or whatever. Imagine our disgust when the Treasury found reason to have a meeting in the third week of the month. Shame! As it turned out the situation was much worse than it seemed. This was positively the last August in the old style. From then on it was work, work, work. Our predecessors just did not know how lucky they were.

Fourth, the opening days of the new Labour government were traumatic for both ministers and civil servants. One of the very earliest ministerial meetings of the new government dealt with some issue about gas from the North Sea. As it happened the two secretaries present were Alex Jarratt and myself. Both of us were on loan from the Ministry of Power and Alex had until very recently been the undersecretary in charge of the gas division of that ministry. That meeting was fairly shambolic because, after 13 years in the wilderness, no minister present had any real knowledge of how the business of Cabinet committees was conducted (there are for example no rules of order of the kind beloved of local authorities and trade unions to which appeal can be made). Of course they learned pretty quickly (but the first encounter with a new world was necessarily a shock) and the three-week election campaign had led to a piling up of a heavy agenda. However, by the luck of the draw Alex and I were able to apply a little intelligent constructive drafting to the minutes so that the final result reflected at least the spirit, if not quite the letter, of the event it purported to describe. At any rate no one complained.

Finally, as a tribute to a great man, may I recall Sir Burke Trend's tenure as Cabinet secretary? A Cabinet secretariat rule was that secretaries always hunted in pairs so as to provide a check on the accuracy of each other's notes. Burke, who was a great teacher and a superb craftsman of the English Language, insisted that this rule be observed even when he was minuting a small gathering of senior ministers. But rather than take an experienced senior colleague with him he almost always summoned one of the junior characters like me to be his partner. Moreover, he stuck to the secretariat practice of each secretary doing the draft of half the text and swapping them for comment and correction. And throughout the whole operation he remained the soul of courtesy and consideration. The learning curve was so steep we got dizzy.

This was the year my father died.

17

The Kitchen: People

President Harry S. Truman was the author of the pungent advice that 'if you can't stand the heat, get out of the kitchen.' He meant the White House but the doctrine holds good for No 10 as well.

My invitation to start sweating came in April 1965 when Sir Laurence Helsby, head of the civil service and permanent secretary at the Treasury, called me in to see him and offered me the job of a private secretary to the prime minister subject to an interview with Mr Wilson. Sir Laurence added, in true Treasury style, that as the move would mean promotion for me I would not receive a private secretary's allowance for the time being. The effect of this, coupled with the impact of tax increases in the budget going through the House at the time, meant that my net pay on promotion rose by the magnificent sum of 20 new pence a month. Nevertheless, I jumped at the chance, the PM and I found we got along and I got the job.

To avoid the confusion that can arise from the plethora of secretaries I mentioned earlier in this saga, I should explain that the private office in No 10 at that time had a pyramid shape. At the top came the principal private secretary (a very bright and dynamic Treasury undersecretary — grade three — named Derek Mitchell); beneath Derek came two private secretaries (in rank assistant secretaries — grade five) — Oliver Wright from the FCO in charge of all overseas and defence issues and myself in charge of all home and parliamentary business. Below us came two assistant private secretaries (in rank principals — grade seven) who helped out generally. We five were all on secondment from line departments on the same principle as applied to Cabinet Office secretaries. The remainder of the No 10 staff comprised the essential 'duty clerks' (young middle managers) who worked shifts and held the machine together round the clock, plus specialists of various kinds including telephonists, communications experts, executives of various kinds, clerks, typists, guards, messengers and drivers. Unlike the committee secretaries these members of staff were mainly attached to No 10 on a permanent basis and stayed in post unless and until they wanted to leave or were promoted out of it.

I arrived at No 10 on the morning of my first day, made myself known to the guards on the front door, and touched hands with my predecessor Philip Woodfield. He introduced me to the rest of the staff and then exploded his bombshell. He had been asked to act as secretary to Earl Mountbatten's mission to the West Indies to look into various aspects of immigration. They were leaving early that afternoon before the PM would be answering parliamentary questions in the House. As I was now in charge of the PM's parliamentary business for the day I had better read the folder. So hail and farewell! I remember nothing of the afternoon's events. But they must have been OK because I am still here aren't I?

From then on I learnt my new job on the run. Exhilarating! And so it went on for three and a half years.

As I have eschewed revealing secrets (not that there are many left now that ex-ministers and advisers have had there say) my stroboscopic lantern will have to return to projecting a flickering light into dark corners.

In this chapter I will deal with purpose and people. Although not visible at first sight the purpose of the private office was, like that of the Cabinet secretariat, to facilitate the decision taking processes of government. We made sure that the prime minister got to the right meetings at the right times and with the correct papers and briefing. We sat in on all meetings involving the PM and listened to all except purely personal telephone calls in order to ensure that any necessary follow up action was taken and that a note for the record went into the archives for future reference. We organized his visitors and looked after their needs. We made sure that, of the mass of paper that flowed through the office by day and by night, the prime minister saw the ones he needed to see in good time and took decisions when these were required. With hindsight we had one considerable advantage over some of our successors in that we, being male with a male PM, could chase ours into the loo if absolutely necessary. In short, we did everything humanly possible to make the wheels of government go round as smoothly as could be managed.

In all this we fulfilled a markedly different role from our Continental counterparts. In France, Germany and many other European administrations (including the Community) the minister's (or commissioner's) 'cabinet' is a personal think-tank and policy-making machine as well as an administrative office. Its members wield a lot of power, tend to arrogance, and sink or swim with the minister they serve. It is a messy system that leads to the politicization of the senior civil service and to debilitating sycophancy.

To my mind, and I think the view is still widely held in Whitehall, the right relationship between civil servant and minister is exemplified by an encounter between a senior minister and a senior official reported to me by a friend who was present. The two elderly (so they seemed then) men sat facing each other with chins jutting out because they could not agree on the right policy to be followed in a particular situation. The official, who had risen through the ranks from the bottom to the top of the service and who did not fear man nor devil, broke the silence.

'OK Minister, you're the boss. Do it your way, but don't say afterwards that I didn't bloody well warn you.'

But let us look at some of the individuals who inhabited No 10 in the mid and late 1960s. I had better begin with the alleged tension between the PM's personal and political secretary, Marcia Williams, and the civil servants of the private office. Sure it existed but it was nothing new and, moreover, was much overdone by a media dominated by sensationalism. (I always treasure the remark by a very senior pressman that the objective of journalists was to sell newspapers and that the British press was at the down-market end of the entertainment industry.) The mundane reality is that every incoming minister finds that about 80 per cent of his time is required by his civil servants for public business and that consequently every personal and political secretary faces a drop in his or her boss's attention time by four-fifths or thereabouts. It should also be noted that, as the taxpayers actually cough up quite handsomely to buy a minister's time, a 20 per cent margin for politics is really quite generous.

Nevertheless, it is inevitably hard for intelligent and committed personal secretaries and advisers to shift into the new mode and to acknowledge that the boss they once cosseted and who occupied so large a place in their lives, is now largely someone else's property. This situation has, of course, arisen many hundreds of times over the years and is soluble by patience, tact and understanding on the part of all concerned — as I think ours was.

To get the other potentially difficult personal situation out of the way at the beginning, Harold Wilson inherited his principal private secretary and much of the rest of the No 10 staff from his predecessor. This was totally normal civil service practice made possible by the apolitical nature of your average civil servant. We were, to use a crude simile, a bit like doorkeepers at a brothel — not particularly surprised at the breadth of the human imagination. Some ministers accepted the position easily. Others took time to settle down. But most managed it in the end. It is worth noting, too, that this problem does not exist in the USA or France. In the former, the spoils go to the victor in the shape of many hundreds of senior civil service and diplomatic jobs. The French as always have their own version in which senior people flit about from being ministers to being officials and back again without seeming pain. But then in republican and egalitarian France the old school (provided it is '*grande*' enough) is the club that matters. A party label is merely a convenient and flexible element in the c.v. I prefer our way.

Of course, by the time a few years had passed our normal rotation system ensured a change in the faces of the private secretaries throughout Whitehall. Moreover, Oliver Cromwell's dictum about being 'willing faithfully to serve' still ruled the roost. Long may it continue to do so! (Though I sometimes, along with others of my generation, fear the worst, may we be proved wrong!)

Among other 'people' matters we got a splendid view from the permanent staff of the habits of previous inhabitants of No 10. A tiny and judicious selection would be:

Mrs Attlee throwing the members of a ministerial committee out of the house at 7.00 p.m. with the terse remark that it was time for her husband to have his dinner.

Her husband, who was also not noted for beating about the bush, when asked by a junior minister why he was being sacked, replying 'because you are no good'.

Harold Macmillan, who had served as a junior infantry officer in the terrible slaughter of Passchendaele, starting a meeting with a group of senior trade unionists about a threatened strike. Half an hour into the meeting they had all, being of the same generation, converted it into a session of wartime reminiscences lubricated by whisky and cigars.

Harold Macmillan, too, taking the trouble to go to the House of Commons in the evening as often as he could to chat with members of any party who happened to be in the smoking room at the time. By doing so, not only could he make his own assessment of feeling in the House but he made a lot of useful cross-party friends as well. Not all of his predecessors or successors were as wise as he and some of them positively invited trouble by being snooty, standoffish or just plain invisible.

As to the denizens of No 10 and its environs during my tenure of office a number of names stand out.

Above all I must pay a fulsome tribute to Joan and Meriel, my indefatigable helpers on parliamentary business. They were bright, friendly, funny and very hardworking. I could not have got through without them.

I should also pay tribute to my two Foreign Office colleagues, Oliver Wright in the first half of my stint and Michael Palliser in the second. Both have many claims to fame but I will ration them to two apiece. Oliver had very dark hair and grew spectacular stubble very quickly. Consequently, his passport photograph looked very sinister indeed and all his friends agreed that, were they immigration officers, they would never let him into the country. With such a handicap his later success in the diplomatic service is even more meritorious. It was also Oliver who used a phrase one day that became our motto: 'Life in No 10 is fine from 9.00 a.m. to 6.00 p.m. but bloody murder from 6.00 p.m. to 9.00 a.m.' 'Too right,' as our Australian friends would say.

As to Michael he must have been, so my wife assures me, a very good-looking young man. He also had a bit of glamour on his c.v., for which most men would give their eye teeth. In 1944, young Palliser commanded a Sherman tank of the Guards armoured division, which he rode from Normandy to Brussels. On arrival he met, and subsequently married,

Marie Spaak, the daughter of Paul-Henri Spaak who later became one of the main architects of the Common Market. 'Gosh!' or even 'Golly!' as Joyce Grenfell would have said.

The other story is a very personal one for me. All prime ministers go abroad a lot taking their FCO private secretary with them. It was also the habit in No 10 for me to remain at home keeping a candle burning in the window. But in early 1968 the PM went to Moscow taking both Michael and me with him. Our adventures on that occasion must be recounted elsewhere but the particular 'bonding' session we experienced ran as follows. Someone in London decided that they had a tale of political intrigue and skulduggery that must go to the PM at once. But, given the peculiar nature of the message, they decided that the only leak-proof method of getting it to him unread by extraneous human eyes was to mark it 'to be deciphered by hand of private secretary only'. In doing so they debarred us, almost certainly unwittingly, from deciphering the message by machine. So, late at night, two lonely figures could be seen huddled over a table covered in paper and cursing gently to each other. Of course, we got through (around dawn as I recall) but only with the help of a whole bottle of splendid Georgian brandy.

It was on this trip, too that the duty clerk accompanying us came away from a visit to the Bolshoi to see *Carmen* with the marvellous crack that despite their superb singing it was the first time he had heard *Carmen* sung by a chorus of lady truck drivers (referring of course to their girth not their occupation). It was on the same visit to the theatre that we noticed that most of the ladies in the audience were wearing the same scarves. On enquiry we were told that they were all members of the communist aristocracy (the *Nomenclatura*) who enjoyed first pick of imported consumer goods and a cargo of Marks & Spencer scarves had just arrived.

There is an informal as well as a formal side to diplomacy. In January 1966 Prime Minister Shastri of India died. From all around the world leading political figures hurried to be present at the funeral — not of course only to pay their respects to the dead leader but also, as Harold Wilson put it, 'to take part in a good working funeral'. The occasion was also memorable for me in that it was the only time in my career that a member of the royal family — Earl Mount-batten — telephoned me at home in the middle of the night. He, like the good sailor he was, was simply checking whether the hastily prepared arrangements for his journey to India as the Queen's representative, still stood.

To round off the foreign theme we had a memorable visit from President Pompidou of France who was invited, among other things, to come to No 10 for lunch. This took place in the state dining room and it was only when everyone had taken their places that we realized that President Pompidou was seated facing three full-length portraits — of Nelson, Wellington and Pitt. Everyone present tried hard not to notice.

Another prominent member of the team at this time was Henry James, the number two in our press office and a very nice man to boot. One day he and the PM were agonizing about some piece of bad news (economic figures probably) that would break on the following day. A common device for dealing with this sort of problem was (and still is) to juggle the publication date of some other item of govern-ment news so as to muffle the impact of the offending piece. But the cupboard was bare and both Henry and the PM had concluded that there was no alternative but to grin and bear it. Come the morning and the front pages were plastered with the story of a particularly gruesome murder. As the two men stared at this gift from the gods the PM turned to Henry and said 'You're a very good fellow Henry, but I didn't expect you to go this far.'

One of my colleagues at No 10, Malcolm Reid, holds a particularly soft spot in our family history. He and his wife, like us, had three sons and both families would have liked a girl to complete the ranks. The Reid's went first and found themselves with a fourth son — Suzanne and I took the hint.

No account of No 10 in the 1960s can sensibly omit devaluation. A fixed rate of exchange was blue murder for the economy (Euro fanatics please note) not least because changes in the exchange rate became dramatic political crises and the process of sudden economic adjustment could be extremely painful. When the government's hand was finally forced the prime minister was much criticized by the opposition for saying that 'the pound in your pocket has not been devalued'. I was present when the offending broadcast was prepared. Amid the chaos of the moment the PM worried that old people might misunderstand 'devaluation' and think that their savings and cash in hand were to be cut in some way. The phrase was intended to reassure them on the point.

Now for George Brown, deputy prime minister in all but formal title, he was the loose cannon of the first Wilson administration. Undoubtedly brilliant in an erratic way, no one really knew the source of his trouble. Some put it down to booze, others, charitably, to an unusual metabolism, yet others saw psychological causes lying deep in the history of the Labour Party. But, whatever the reason, George was his own worst enemy and much given to trying to get his way by childlike threats to resign. Inevitably, the day came when his resignation was taken at its face value and he was out. It was sad.

Among other regular attendees of note at No 10 were, Ernie Fernyhough MP, the PM's parliamentary private secretary, who acted as his personal representative with the party's backbench MPs and who helped out with the PM's parliamentary chores; his successors, Gerald Kaufman and Eric Varley, who both went on to enjoy distinguished ministerial careers; Tommy Balogh the Hungarian economist and long-time friend of the PM; George Wigg, the paymaster general and very close confidant of the PM; and Arnold Goodman, the PM's personal lawyer.

Ernie was MP for Jarrow, one of the Labour Party's safest seats in the House. He was a trade union MP of the old (and very loyal) school and a charming and unpretentious human being with a vast circle of friends and acquaintances in the party and the trade union movement. One little story may give the flavour of the man. The day the general election of 1966 was announced I bumped into him and said that I supposed he would now be very busy in his constituency. 'Oh no,' he replied 'my majority is enormous and safe. I will now be enjoying myself making speeches on behalf of my less fortunate friends in their constituencies. It's great fun and earns me a lot of Brownie points.'

Of the other PPSs, Gerald Kaufman added to his other talents that of the writer of one of the funniest books on politics I know, *How to be a Minister*. If ever I am asked to devise a training course for would-be ministers that will be one of my recommended textbooks.

Next, I must say a word about the PM's good friend and adviser, George Wigg who at this time was paymaster general. The PM was on holiday in the Scilly Isles when news came through that a madman with a gun was loose and probably seeking to assassinate him. I was on duty at the time and George and I pressed every button we could think of to ensure the PM's safety. Finally, there came a lull in the proceedings and George, who had a mischievous turn of mind, looked at me with a twinkle in his eye and his tongue firmly in his cheek, and said 'You know Peter I don't care if someone does shoot the PM. What concerns me is what my actions will look like at the court of inquiry afterwards.' There spoke a true ex-sergeant of the British army.

And, forever joined in my mind with George Wigg was Tommy Balogh. I say joined because they not only shared an intense loyalty for the PM but were also forever wrangling about how best to protect the PM's interests. It made very good, if private, theatre.

Finally, there was Arnold Goodman. He was present at a

reception one evening when the conversation turned to the hoary old subject of the split of the legal profession between solicitors and barristers (Arnold was, of course, a solicitor). Did he not find this split inconvenient? 'No,' he replied without hesitation, 'when I need a barrister I hire one.'

So much for prominent individuals. In addition, No 10, like all good institutions, was blessed with a superb support staff. Small in numbers for the jobs they had to do, but too many to spell out by name, they all — middle managers, clerks, typists, security men, messengers, drivers, cleaners and so on — made an unbeatable contribution to the smooth running of the centre of British government. It would be invidious to pick out for special mention any individual or group within the support staff but, lest I should be accused of forgetfulness, I readily acknowledge the immense debt we all owed to the ladies who managed our switchboard. Their reputation for superb service was legendary. Indeed, it was said of them that if you wanted to talk to a Mr John Brown, thought to be resident in the United States of America you had but to ask and they would find the right one. I was in their debt a thousand times but one very good test of their prowess came on the Sunday morning when the tanker named *Torrey Canyon* failed to miss the Scilly Isles. I was the duty dog and found myself trying to cope in a situation where everything was happening too fast for me to break away from home to go to the office where staff, kit and information were available to ease the task. Instead, there was I, sitting on the floor at home with my scrambler telephone, trying to make sure that everything that should happen did happen. The technique we invented was for the switchboard to phone me and keep the line open unless and until I agreed to accept an incoming call. In handling all this I was much aided by having an excited prime minister on the phone every five minutes from his perch on the cliffs of St Mary's giving me a blow by blow account of developments. The emergency services were most impressed by the speed with which No 10 kept abreast of what was going on.

AN EXCITED PRIME MINISTER ON THE PHONE EVERY FIVE MINUTES

18

The Kitchen: Parliament

It is now time to turn our attention to Parliament. At that time the PM was obliged to answer parliamentary questions, live, twice a week (on Tuesday and Thursday afternoons) plus, of course, PQs for written answer. Altogether in my three and a half years in the job I organized the answers to around five thousand questions plus many thousands of possible answers to supplementary questions. There was also a whole raft of private notice questions to cope with (PNQs are questions for which a minister gets precious little warning, dealing with some urgent topic that has arisen unexpectedly) together with the need to deal with debates and to keep a close eye on what was going on in other corners of the parliamentary jungle. Oddly enough it was great fun and fitted in neatly with both my academic and practical experience.

In the course of my duties I spent a great deal of time in the House of Commons (usually in the little box in which officials can sit to the left of the speaker's chair as seen from the floor of the House). Technically, this box is outside the chamber but is close enough to the action for officials to be able to pass bits of paper to the MPs sitting in front of them for onward transmission to whichever minister needs help. From this vantage point I had a grandstand view of events. Moments to treasure were:

- The moment when, with only a tiny government majority, a backbench member slid to the ground with a heart attack. Two or three doctors in the House rushed to his aid. Almost everyone else dug out their Vacher's and looked up his majority. As it happened he survived.
- The moment when George Thomas, later one of Parliament's most famous speakers, but then secretary of state for Wales, answered a PQ with what the MP who had asked it called 'a most wriggling sort of answer'. Unabashed, George shot back 'of course it was; it was a very wriggling sort of question' — to get the full flavour of George's reply, it has to be said out loud with some approximation to his Welsh accent.
- The moment when George Brown turned over two pages in his PQ folder so that the answer bore absolutely no relationship to the question that had been asked. Much rustling of papers in the House as (some) members woke up. Then George realized what had happened and said, in a stentorian voice, 'Mr Speaker I've got a better answer here.'
- The day when George Wigg tried out his new theory (afterwards abandoned) that all PQs could be answered with a simple 'yes' or a 'no' — a belief I think founded on the accepted doctrine that hostile newsmen or women are best fended off with monosyllabic answers because they rapidly run out of their researcher's prepared questions. The trouble was not only that he and his fellow MPs soon got thoroughly muddled but also that the premise proved wrong. (Try answering 'yes' to the question 'how many'.)
- The day the PM was opening a debate on foreign affairs (I think on Vietnam) when events were moving fast and the telegrams were pouring in. Consequently, he was amending his speech up to the last moment in his room in the House and the typists, good though they were, had difficulty in keeping up. The upshot was that the PM

was on his feet speaking before the typing was complete and fresh sheets were fed to him along the bench from the aforementioned official box as they were completed and checked. At last he came to the end and sat down looking remarkably unflustered. Not so the No 10 team who collapsed behind the scenes.

Before we leave number 10, I will reveal a secret. Harold Wilson had a very good memory; the House knew it and he exploited it. Thus his off the cuff answers in debate or at question time were liberally sprinkled with phrases like 'I dealt with that fully in the debate we had on 12 January last. I think it is recorded at about column 218 of *Hansard* for that day.' Or, 'As I have told the honourable member several times, most recently about six months ago, it was I think on a wet Wednesday afternoon, that story is much exaggerated.' If only the lazy ninnies had had the gumption to check they would have found the answers were not quite as crushing as they appeared. As George Wigg used to complain so often, too many MPs did not 'do their 'omework' as assiduously as they should have done.

Next I should mention an interesting development in parliamentary procedure that happened during my tenure of office. The House of Commons had long had a powerful committee among its weapons for holding the executive responsible for its actions — the Public Accounts Committee. This committee, heavily weighted with MPs who were accountants or lawyers by training, scrutinized the government's accounts and cross-examined ministers and officials about them. The PAC had a professional staff at its disposal, headed, then, by the comptroller and auditor general, and had acquired a fearsome reputation in Whitehall. But, unlike the Congress of the USA, Parliament had few other committees to supervise the government's conduct of public business. To its credit the Labour government of my day began to establish committees that would eventually shadow every major department of state. Unfortunately, the system, while useful as a means of obtaining information, did not live up to the hopes of some of its founders. Government found it irksome to be criticized and both the honours' system and the prospect of future office in government proved a powerful disincentive to candour or free ranging enquiry. (It is not a coincidence that the office of prime minister evolved from that of the early eighteenth-century post of 'patronage secretary'.) Moreover, of course, the nature of our parliamentary democracy takes many of the best and brightest MPs from the government benches out of the field of recruitment for committee membership. However, a start was made and perhaps some day either a government will give the committees real freedom or the backbenchers of all parties will use their overwhelming latent power to force their will on government — as they have so successfully done in respect of their own pay and perks.

Modern life is afflicted by machinery in many forms and the life of an MP is governed by a simple electric bell — the one that tells him that the House of Commons is about to vote and that he has just eight minutes to get to the chamber if his vote is to be recorded. The 'division bells' as they are called are scattered throughout the Palace of Westminster and in adjacent buildings, including No 10 Downing Street. When the government's majority is slim it is vital that every party member, including the prime minister, registers his or her vote. This situation prevailed during part of my tenure in Downing Street and led to some pretty hairy moments. I particularly recall an afternoon when the United Nations Association had been invited to hold a garden party in the grounds of No 10. In the course of this event we were warned that a division (vote) was to take place unexpectedly. The PM was told but decided not to inconvenience the guests by calling off his planned speech to them. Instead, we arranged for one of the No 10 cars to be waiting outside the front door with the engine running and the driver behind the wheel. Soon afterwards the bells 'went down', as the wartime fire service used to say. As it happened, the PM was in mid-speech when I signalled to him. A very hasty 'thank you all for coming' and the PM and I ran like blazes through the house, into the car and away with squealing tyres (the two No 10 drivers were both highly accomplished ex-members of the police flying squad). A burst of speed to Parliament Square, into Palace Yard, out we both tumbled, a quick sprint up the stairs to the Commons chamber and Mr Wilson made it with seconds to spare. I had long maintained that the main qualification for the job of prime minister is stamina. That afternoon proved it.

Finally, I should mention a parliamentary mystery. The question of parliamentary privilege has dominated the life of Parliament since its earliest days. And the essence of privilege is the freedom of members to speak and act without constraint in the interests of their constituents. Given this, a large question mark will be seen to hang over the techniques of party discipline currently practised in Parliament. And, indeed, whenever I raised this issue privately with MPs I was told that this was the reason for the wording of the instructions sent to all members by their party managers each week in the so-called 'whip', namely requesting their attendance rather than their vote for particular bits of parliamentary business. To tell them how to vote would, I was assured, fall foul of parliamentary privilege. Unfortunately, none of the books I have consulted (including the parliamentary Bible, Erskine May) give anything approaching a straight answer to a straight question on the issue. I offer this free as a suitable subject for research by any MP who feels suicidal or any Ph.D. student who wishes to improve his c.v.

19

The Kitchen: The Civil Service

Half way through my time at No 10 the government decided to set up a committee under the chairmanship of Lord Fulton 'to examine the structure, recruitment and management, including training, of the Home Civil Service and to make recommendations'. Before looking at the results of the work of the Fulton Committee it may be helpful if I sketch in briefly the historical origins of our present civil service. For the first 600 years of our history after the Norman Conquest our country was run by the monarch of the day as if it were his or her private estate. The king or queen collected the taxes, paid the bills and hired the servants needed to run the show. Parliament existed as a forum for sanctioning or refusing new laws and taxes but real discussion of government business was reserved for the monarch's private (hence 'Privy') Council, whose members were chosen by the monarch and who were solely responsible to him or her.

The Civil War of the 1640s, the republic of the 1650s and the Glorious Revolution of 1688 changed all that. Parliament ran the country throughout the Civil War and acquired a taste for power that never left it. The Restoration worked because both king and Parliament recognized that the old world of the 'divine right of kings' had died with Charles I on the scaffold in Whitehall. And when James II tried to put the clock back he was thrown out on his ear. The reign of William and Mary and the expensive wars with France cemented the post-revolution partnership between Crown and Parliament. The death of Queen Anne without an heir in 1714 (despite having borne 18 children) opened the way for the final supremacy of Parliament. The Hanoverians were brought in, virtually on contract, to handle the ceremonial side of the monarchy, the Cabinet took control of policy under the prime minister and each department of state hired its own employees.

Despite its faults this system endured until the mid-nineteenth century. After all, it may have lost us the American colonies but it beat Napoleon didn't it? But the spirit of the age was reformist; the inadequacies of the old regime were easy to parody (a Treasury notice to staff in the 1840s is alleged to have read something like 'staff are reminded that the hours of attendance are from ten until four and that a line will be drawn across the attendance book at 11.00 a.m. sharp.') Moreover, the experience of the East India Company in creating and running the growing Indian Empire showed that it was perfectly possible to recruit, train and manage a highly professional civil service fully capable of performing the tasks required of it. 'So if they can do it', said the Whitehall mandarins of the day, 'why can't we?'

Two reports showed the way forward. The Macaulay Report showed how the East India Company recruited its senior staff by competitive examination and went deeply into the nature of the examination required. The Northcote–Trevelyan Report put forward a damning critique of the old system of recruitment, including such splendid judgements as 'Admission into the civil service is eagerly sought after but it is for the unambitious, and the indolent or incapable, that it is chiefly desired.' And again the report went on to say that civil servants 'may obtain an honourable livelihood with little labour and no risk' and in jobs 'where their success depends upon their simply avoiding any flagrant misconduct, and attending with moderate regularity to routine duties'. Phew!

Fortunately, the report then went on to say that 'there are numerous honourable exceptions to these observations' and that 'they', namely civil servants in general, 'are much better than we have any right to expect from the system under which they are recruited and promoted'. The report's final judgement argued in favour of a unified civil service, with a single entrance examination for all departments and for complete mobility between departments for the more junior staff. Both reports (which the interested reader will find reproduced in full in Annex B to the Fulton Report) were masterpieces of compressed common sense and both greatly influenced the pattern of civil service development over the next 100 years.

Incidentally, it is interesting to note that the Northcote–Trevelyan Report not only successfully advocated centralized recruitment based on the guiding principle of 'fair and open competition' but rejected the idea of promotion by merit on the grounds that to embrace it would encourage nepotism, favouritism and corruption. What, I wonder, do today's civil servants (who have a reasonably impartial system for promotion but have to live with its second cousin, merit pay) think of these old arguments?

But let us get back to Fulton. The committee reported in June 1968 and its report proved to be the most thorough and radical review of the Home Civil Service since the aforementioned Northcote–Trevelyan Report of 1853. This is not the place to examine the Fulton Report in depth but any student with a mind to explore the matter further will find it a very readable document. In the event, the government accepted many, but not all, of the committee's recommendations, even though implementation took many years and is not yet complete. Indeed, some of the changes made, for example the creation of a civil service department responsible for most staffing matters, were implemented and then reversed. Others, for example the endorsement by Fulton of the then existing pay determination system based on 'fair comparisons', did not save that system from abolition later. And the major change of the 1990s, for example the creation of an organizational system based on 'agencies', only appeared in Fulton as a reference to the Swedish system of the same name. It should also be noted that the English version of the agency concept was a weak and feeble thing compared with its Scandinavian namesake. Indeed, our version might be thought by a cynic to be designed to increase the distance between ministers and the actions of their employees without the surrender of real power. The days of Critchel Down — with the minister accepting personal responsibility for (and resigning because of) the failures of his ministry — are truly behind us now.

From the point of view of my closing days at No 10 the immediate impact of Fulton lay in the controversy it aroused. For example, the left wing of the Labour Party crowed loudly about the Fulton recommendation to abolish 'classes' in the civil service. As so often in politically motivated arguments of this kind, the quiet voices of reason pointed out that this was a question of semantics and that the British civil service actually enjoyed a higher degree of upward mobility than virtually any other in the world (about half of senior jobs for grade sevens and above were filled by promotees from the lower ranks). Similarly, the charge of 'amateurism' levelled by many at the senior civil servants of the day was felt by some of us to be not unconnected with the ambitions of some academics to make money by taking over the training of civil servants in their university departments. But be that as it may, it was fun to be at the centre of things at that seminal time for my profession.

Envoi

Finally, I should record one happy memory of No 10 of a totally non-political kind. The house is very conveniently situated overlooking Horse Guards Parade and its windows give a grandstand view of events like the trooping of the colour. Each year the PM used to invite friends and families of the staff to come along and share the view of events like that. My children, now of course well and truly grown up, still recall careering around the house with lots of other children and stuffing themselves with coke, biscuits, cakes and ice cream.

WHEN THE RIVER BURST ITS BANKS

But all good things have to come to an end and September 1968 found me on my way out. The event was doubly notable because we lived in Hurst Park, upriver a little from Hampton Court, and were subjected to a major flood when the River Mole burst its banks. Our house, which we had just been about to sell, had goldfish swimming in the living room and many less pleasant objects floating about. Nevertheless, we made it (just) to the farewell party organized for us by the PM but I am afraid that I had so much on my mind that I made a very poor fist of my parting speech. But everyone was very kind to Suzanne and me and, while a lifelong subscriber to the belief that 'big boys don't cry,' I could very easily have broken the club rules on that occasion.

20

Last Port Before the Storm

D amp, tired but happy I reported back to the Ministry of Power to find that my splendid PEO (by now Bernard Gottlieb) had found me a temporary billet in which to catch my breath after too much excitement. This was in our petroleum division dealing with all aspects of international oil policy. In this role I became the UK's 'oil' representative at both the EEC and the OECD. This was my first semi-independent overseas post (albeit I remained based in London) and my first real contact with the newly-concentrated Brussels machine (the three previously independent parts of the European Community — Common Market, Coal and Steel and Euratom — had been formally merged in 1965 and most Community business was now centred in Brussels). Neither post was onerous as we only had observer status in Brussels and the OECD energy work was still at the analytical level and was to remain so until the Yom Kippur War.

Nevertheless, the contacts I made and the operational feel I gained of the two organizations stood me in good stead in the years immediately ahead. But for the moment my task was to find my way about and I enjoyed myself testing cheap hotels, restaurants and office canteens, so as to ease the task of living within the Treasury's fixed daily subsistence allowance. Incidentally, the EEC routine in those days was for Commission minions to appear (very discreetly) during the morning session of a committee and hand out little brown envelopes containing the delegates' travel and subsistence allowances in cash to all those present except the Brits. Our money went instead direct to the Treasury, which dealt with our allowances in its own way and made, we all believed, a good profit on the deal. Indeed, I think this operation was the first sign of the Treasury coming to terms with commercial practice. They even made a deal to book cut-price rooms at the, then rather aged, Hotel Metropole in Brussels. I am sorry to have to report, however, that it took them a very long time to get round to screwing the airlines, despite being pressed to do so by characters like me.

I had only been doing this job for a few months when the Ministry of Power did some internal reorganization and I found myself in the catch-all dustbin of general division. Luckily, my new duties subsumed my old; however, I also had added responsibility for subjects like district heating (one of those technical quick fixes beloved of politicians) and (shades of the future) civil emergency planning (which theoretically embraced natural disasters but realistically meant strikes).

Once again I had barely got my feet under the table when the Ministry of Power was wound up and merged into the Ministry of Technology under its flamboyant minister, Tony Benn. There was again a change of name for the division to the fuel and nationalized industry policy division. My duties were again unchanged except that responsibility was added for coordinating energy investment. I was getting busy again at a rate of knots but once more fate intervened. The Conservatives, under Ted Heath, won the general election in June 1970 and, among other things, set up the super new Department of Trade and Industry into which MinTech was shovelled. It took time for the new ministry to settle down and for the time being my job remained unchanged except that my civil emergencies' role embraced the whole department. As an indication of how big the place was, any notes I sent out about the industrial relations scene needed to go to 65 separate addressees.

It was in this job too that I learned what the ham in a sandwich feels like. Moira Denehy, a distinguished lady undersecretary who was a chain smoking dynamo, retired from the service and found very rapidly indeed that inactivity was desperately boring. Three weeks out from the retirement speeches she was hammering on the door of the Civil Service Commission demanding to be found a job. And shortly thereafter she was re-employed as a temporary principal (three steps down the pyramid from her previous rank) and posted to fill a vacancy working for me. Moira played a potentially difficult situation with great skill but I was always aware that she had forgotten more about administration than I ever knew. She also had the sort of personality, honed by many years of Whitehall infighting, that enabled her to crush her opponents in debate and negotiation, especially if they were men. She was particularly effective abroad where, not only were most of our foreign counterparts male, but most had never before had to do business with an intelligent, ruthless and quite unscrupulous Anglo-Saxon female old enough to be their grandmother and clutching a tin of 50 cigarettes in one hand and her personal ashtray in the other.

As it happened my real boss was also an undersecretary. He was an intelligent Welshman who was verbose where Moira was taciturn and whose output of paper must have contributed to global warming. His strongest point was an ability to engage in the minutiae of complex argument; Moira's was an ability to say 'no' endlessly for as long as it took to make her opponents understand the meaning of the word.

Moira also had a secret weapon hidden in the bottom left hand drawer of her desk — a collection of useful, striking, or otherwise distinguished bits of text culled from passing minutes and newspapers, which, she alleged, enabled her to cobble together a minute on any subject without further thought. Very useful!

Looking back, the three muddled years between leaving No 10 and the next big change in my career, which occurred in 1971, appear to have little real substance for me. But in them we joined the Common Market and set out on the road that led, eventually, to Margaret Thatcher's revolution. From then on the pace of my life, together with that of my country, really began to hot up.

* * *

Early in 1970, as if to dig in before the battle, we finally sold our flood benighted house at a loss and moved to the cheaper end of Esher very near to a middle-class comprehensive school. Given the lunacies of education policies in those days the only ways to avoid the (many) junk state schools was to be rich enough to pay for private education (which we were not) or to move into a catchment area with better state schools. Our new house was big, solid and with a garden large enough for small boys to play football (or bang bangs) in.

21

The Quick Fix

The reader will remember that my early permanent
secretaries were survivors of the battles of the First
World War. Now the ranks were beginning to fill
with the survivors of the second. Among them was the permanent secretary of the new DTI — Sir Anthony Part —
who had been one of a small band of junior officers
gathered together by Sir Bernard Montgomery (as he then
was) to act as his eyes and ears when he commanded the
Eighth Army in the North African desert.

One afternoon soon after the merger I was sent for by
Anthony and told that he intended to promote me to undersecretary and put me in charge of the regional industrial
development division. In this job I would be responsible for
all industrial aspects of regional development including the
administration of the local employment acts — which provided *inter alia* for making loans and grants for industrial
development; industrial development certificates (IDCs); and
the supervision of the industrial estates corporations. In this
situation I would be at the hub of some pretty vicious interdepartmental infighting as a number of powerful bees
gathered round a rather small honey pot. I would also need
to consider the regional implications of entry into the Common Market, which loomed steadily larger in our planning.

Having explained all this and told me that my new
division had 300 staff and a budget of a good many million

pounds, Anthony went on to say 'However good the help I have, this ministry is far too big for one man to keep a close eye on everything that goes on. My method of control is, therefore, to make you and your fellows totally responsible for doing your jobs properly. If anything goes wrong I will fall on you like a ton of bricks. Good luck!'

I then went off to say goodbye to my old troops and hello to the new ones before moving into my new office in 1 Victoria Street.

On reviewing the tasks of my division it quickly became clear that my main problem in Whitehall would be to hold the ring between the various regional interests involved and, more widely, to cope with the financial implications of a largely discretionary system.

On the first issue I knew that my Cabinet Office experience would help a lot and that I would have to build on the old office's reputation for fairness between its customers. To this end I decided to capitalize on my Channel Islands ancestry (as we did not give the islanders any money I might escape a charge of favouritism). I also recalled the old story of the Jesuit priest who was called upon to decide a dispute between the Benedictines and another monastic order about which of their houses God most favoured. The judgement was 'You are all equal in my sight' signed 'God SJ'. The implication I tried to convey was that, to us piratical southerners, the lands north of Alderney were all equally labelled 'HERE BE DRAGONS'.

As for the rest of my task I knew that the bulk of the staff effort was consumed in applying the local employment acts. These acts, containing powers to give discretionary financial help to new industrial investments in the development areas (broadly speaking most of Scotland, Wales and northern England) represented a succession of past laws that had been introduced and partly abandoned as governments changed. Indeed, substantial numbers of my staff were engaged in winding up the past, in the form of ongoing servicing of old cases, rather than coping with the future. From my point of view, however, the real bugbear was that the powers in the LEAs were discretionary. This opened a wide field of potential corruption for the civil servants and a great temptation to lie for the applicants. After all, as one of my older hands said, it is a lottery in which you invest six pence in a stamp and may get a million pounds back by way of a loan or grant from government — good odds. The potential corruption at our end we could (and already did) cope with by the usual methods — identify the danger points; put yourselves in the mind of the potential briber and bribe taker; and then construct the administrative machine so that success in delivering the goods to the criminal faces diminished opportunities and heightened risks. An example is the practice of the customs and excise department of shifting its officers around the country frequently in order that the opportunities for building a long-term relationship with the local baddies is much reduced. I think we succeeded in this endeavour though, as experience in other countries has shown, there are lots of people around willing to take risks for what may be seen as easy profits. Moreover, once the corruption bug has taken hold in an area where government funds swill around in quantity or valuable rights are on offer, it becomes very difficult to eradicate. The trick is to identify the areas of highest risk (for example regional or overseas aid — the latter being, I suspect, the currently most rewarding honey pot) and to concentrate on them.

The potential corruption of the applicants was more difficult to handle because the honest had to suffer delay along with the dishonest while we checked up as best we could. Moreover, many of the dishonest (or the wildly optimistic or the nutters) were adept at enlisting local, and especially political, support by trading on legitimate local concerns about unemployment and the uncertainties of the future. Add to this a natural desire on the part of ministers to say 'yes' when any voter, or potential voter, wanted a 'goody' and the total inability of anyone to prove (as successive critics pointed out) that the developments we aided would not have taken place anyway, and it was clear that, while the political dividends were self-evident, the cost effectiveness of our efforts was, to say the least, 'not proven'.

The government's industrial estates corporations were to local politics what 'assisted area boundaries' were to regional politics — good for a headline when the going got rough. Essentially, they were industrial estates where government could and did build small factories in advance of demand. They, and the favourable rents that went with them, could then be used to tempt entrepreneurs to set up shop in areas of surplus labour. Again no one knew if these factories actually increased employment in a given area or simply shifted it around. But, whether they did or not, they were a potent symbol of what today is known as, rather sickeningly for my taste, 'caring' and they certainly looked better than the wasteland they usually replaced.

For the rest one story must suffice. Unemployment figures always rise in the winter and are a potent weapon in the misleading exchange of raw data, which so often passes for political argument. Thus, in tabloid terms, most winters see an unemployment 'crisis' and, in my day, this required governments to appear active. A favourite gimmick of the time was for governments to institute 'winter works programmes' to combat rising unemployment. (Incidentally, it is one of the wonders of the age how many military terms have become embedded in political rhetoric — terms like 'combat', 'attack', 'campaign' and 'battle'. It is perhaps the most durable part of Lenin's legacy.) The real problem about these programmes was that capital expenditure, which was their staple diet, cannot be turned on and off like a tap. For instance, 'competitive tendering' was slowly (and rightly) replacing 'cost plus' and it is virtually impossible to create and launch a programme of new capital investment in a matter of weeks. So the Treasury mandarin who came to me bearing a cheque for £25 million, which I could have provided I spent it all in the coming six months, knew what he was doing — and so did I. I was proved right well into the future when many of my requests for Treasury cash provoked the slick retort, 'but you once turned down a cheque for £25 million.'

Supervision of the issue of IDCs — akin to the issue of planning permission for private and commercial projects — was also fraught with problems. For one thing the system provided no bar (nor could it provide such a bar except at a prohibitive cost in compensation) on the reuse of existing buildings. Thus, it did not prevent a number of new industrial projects from seeking to come to prosperous areas. It merely ensured that either they were shoehorned into unsuitable, and therefore inefficient, premises, or went overseas. For another thing, because the IDCs related to a specific place and project, they dragged the government into massive internal squabbles between the different development areas. Moreover, the bidding process between, say, Wales, Scotland, Northern Ireland (all separately represented in Cabinet by senior ministers with industrial development powers) and northern England (not separately represented but politically important) tended to raise the ante in cash terms and heightened the probability that the final outcome would be sub-optimal in terms of both financial and industrial logic. It also imposed long, and costly delays on the completion of the projects themselves. In short, the fourth strip mill syndrome became part of the British disease.

In the years immediately before 1971 there had been a spate of major industrial collapses, like those of Rolls-Royce and Upper-Clyde Shipbuilders, which had not only required rescue by the government but had also needed primary legislation to give effect to their *de facto* nationalization. Such legislation took a great deal of parliamentary time and diverted much ministerial and official effort from normal duties.

There was, therefore, growing pressure for reform of the system of aiding our older industrial areas as well as 'lame duck' industries and firms. Moreover, as entry into the Common Market became closer and more certain, there was a growing realization that British industry was in far from a fit state to face unprotected competition from our European partners. In particular, there was a widespread fear that our industry still lagged behind our competitors in the volume and effectiveness of its capital investments. Quick action here was seen as necessary if lost ground were to be made up.

So it was that, not long after taking office, the new Conservative government of 1970 set in train a very high level (and very secret) review by officials of these connected issues. The review was given the code name of 'Cockaigne' (no doubt reflecting the musical tastes of the PM and Sir William Armstrong, the then head of the Treasury). All those taking part (including me as the responsible under-secretary in the DTI) were warned of the need for absolute secrecy — to the point that even our immediate staffs were not to be informed of the reason for our frequent disappearances from our offices. We worked hard through and beyond the Christmas period and the results of our labours, and equally secret ministerial meetings, emerged as a white paper issued in March 1972. Legislation followed soon after.

The underlying theme of our work was that we needed a relatively simple and, so far as possible, automatic system of criteria for allocating funds to bolster capital investment in manufacturing industry. To this end all claims were classified by location (which determined the percentage of the investment costs that could be reimbursed) and the 'standard industrial classification' of the project (which determined whether the costs were reimbursable at all). We hired extra staff to handle the work at local level and the whole machine swung into action as soon as the Industry Act (1972) came into force.

At the last minute (namely just before the white paper was published) I went to Brussels to tell DGIV (the competition directorate) of our plans. They sucked their teeth at the self-evident bounce, but raised no formal objection.

One final point was that the new DTI, as Anthony Part had said, was too big to be controlled by one man. It also had, inevitably, no single corpus of doctrine and no sense of unity. Left to itself it would have remained essentially composed of the separate ministries from which it had been formed. Anthony's solution to this problem was simple. No member of staff could be transferred or promoted to another job in his old department. Mixing would be inevitable and compulsory. It is a great pity that the new department was just beginning to shake down into a single entity when fate took a decisive hand in our affairs.

22

The European Development Fund

B ut before we tackle fate in the shape of the Yom Kippur War let us take another look at the EEC. At about this time the British government let it be known that, should our new bid for membership of the Community be accepted, it would seek to use regional policy in the Community to claw back part of the outrageous burden we were expected to bear through the financing of the CAP (Common Agricultural Policy) and adverse effects of the Common Fisheries Policy we had been bounced into accepting in the closing stages of the negotiating process. The point was accepted in principle by our partners though no firm commitments were entered into by them. Naturally enough the process of negotiation about the regional fund could not really get underway until agreement on our entry had been achieved and a date for entry accepted by all. Nevertheless, work began and Roy Denman, head of the European unit in the Cabinet Office and I, as head of the industrial development division of the DTI, became more and more embroiled as the key dates approached. Incidentally, to jump ahead a little, as the actual negotiations got underway in 1973 Roy and I, who (it appears to be accepted) made a good team, toured Europe talking to our counterparts in the other member countries. We knew we were doing it right when someone in the Foreign Office asked if we could be restrained from clumping around Europe in hobnailed boots.

This brings me to a point that needs to be made somewhere if the relationship of the UK and the Community is to be properly understood. This can be summed up in the old Whitehall jibe that 'the Foreign Office is a department whose self-imposed task is to represent the interests of foreigners in the UK Cabinet.' Such a view exaggerates a little but not much. The point is that the Foreign Office has seen its role for many years as the not dishonourable one of being to preserve peace among our neighbours by an endless search for compromise and conciliation. The habit of mind engendered by such a search can only too often slip into a belief that any treaty is better than no treaty and any agreement is better than no agreement. Oddly enough, the same mindset grips the Treasury except that, in its case, the goal is to save money irrespective of the merits of the activity thereby starved of funds.

Luckily for the rest of us the consequences of Treasury parsimony hurt voters directly and through them politicians. Some, at any rate, of the Treasury's follies can therefore be overcome before too much damage is done to individuals or the economy at large. Unfortunately, the consequences of the FCO's follies are more likely to emerge too late to allow corrective action. Moreover, too many ministers exposed to foreign blandishments, flattery and threats find themselves temperamentally in the ranks of the appeasers (I believe that the average politician's private prayer is 'please, God, make everyone love me.') And, as we have seen too often since we joined the Community, an inability to say 'no' and mean it can be catastrophic in that den of thieves.

On the other hand the diplomatic service of our French neighbours has no such handicap. Their remit is simple. 'If it is good for France do it, if not stop it or sell it for something that is.' It is also clear that an ability to sell a spavined horse to an Irish tinker and a willingness to rob a blind man without remorse, are traits highly prized by the personnel department of the Quai d'Orsay. I am not sure what the remedy is short of manning the FCO with staff on short-term secondment from the tougher economic departments or of withdrawing the FCO altogether from Europe and replacing it with representatives drawn from these departments and grouped together in a new department headed by a dyspeptic Euro-sceptic minister. And, as a first step, perhaps we should put statues of General Charles de Gaulle and Vyacheslav ('Old Stone Bottom') Molotov in the lobby of the FCO as a permanent reminder of the power of the negative.

A PERMANENT REMINDER OF THE POWER OF THE NEGATIVE

Oddly enough, with running a big division with a massive case load; implementing the new powers of the Industry Act; aiding ministers with parliamentary business, visiting deputations and crises; and rushing around Europe my three

years in the industrial development division were so frantic-
ally busy that my recollections of life in those days are even
more fragmented than usual. However, a few highlights are
worth recording.

The weekly meeting of ministers and senior staff took
place in the main conference room of our Victoria Street
offices. Between 30 and 40 people were present and the
usual routine was to hear statements of progress on topical
issues, followed by a presentation in depth of one area of
ministry policy made by the responsible under or deputy
secretary. It was a very challenging experience because the
audience knew its stuff and proof, if proof were needed, that
the 'super ministry' was basically too big.

There was an occasion when one of my assistant secretaries passed incorrect information to our secretary of state
John Davies, a very bright man brought into government
from the CBI and a political innocent. The S. of S. used the
duff information in the House and was subsequently chal-
lenged as to its accuracy. He then faced the humiliation of
having to stand up before a totally silent House and apologize. Once seen never forgotten.

Chris Chataway (my immediate minister) and I going to a
secret meeting in Sussex with a commissioner and some of
his staff from Brussels to talk about regional policy was very
melodramatic (the Brussels contingent flew in by private
plane) but pretty useless. However, I suppose it massaged a
few egos (*not* the minister's or mine. We were fireproof).

Again, the minister and I went to see the PM at No 10
about a meeting on regional policy scheduled to take place
in Brussels. Imagine the scene with the Cabinet room empty
apart from the PM and a private secretary sitting in the centre
of the coffin-shaped cabinet table with their backs to the
fireplace and Chris and me sitting immediately opposite
them. The PM was holding forth with a rather bad tempered
monologue largely, as I recall, centring on the alleged sins of
Commission officials interpreting the treaty in ways the UK

did not find congenial. It was an early lesson in the realities of the legal morass we now found ourselves in.

There is one more story involving Chris Chataway. A television company was making a series of programmes about decision taking in government. We had been invited to take part in one about the way parliamentary questions were dealt with. So, after a sweat to find a wholly innocuous question (in those days people took parliamentary privilege seriously), the cameras came to my house to film me at my usual routine of dealing with official papers lying on the carpet. It was a successful operation apart from the heat of the lights burning a dark patch in my ceiling — for which I was offered £10 in compensation. The scene then switches to the minister's room in the Office. Seated around the table were the minister, his private secretary, one of my staff and me. After filming a few words about the PQ in question the producer said 'If you've finished with this one we'll leave you to get on with the rest.' 'Phooey,' said my boss. 'We don't normally go through all this garbage. We just put it on for your benefit.' So much for documentaries and flies on the wall!

One other memory of a minister will bear recounting. This relates to John Eden who was minister for industry in the DTI from 1970 to 1972. Sometime in this period he paid an official visit to Dundee and I went with him as the regional undersecretary. As we were about to enter a building where our next meeting was to be held, we found our way barred by a mob of yelling demonstrators, ostensibly protesting about unemployment. John, who was an ex-Ghurkha officer, with all the qualities of that breed, stepped into the middle of the crowd, politely took the microphone from the cheer leader, and gave a brief but pointed summary of all the government was trying to do to improve the economic situation. The crowd quietened down, some even clapped, and we went inside for our meeting. When we came out the crowd had gone.

Of my many trips to Brussels at this time a good number brought me into contact with a large Italian who was the Commission's director general of regional policy. He was a splendid man although, like a good many Continentals, a bit of a hypochondriac. These meetings usually ended with an invitation to lunch with my friend. One day, looking sad, he waved at the menu and said 'Have anything you like Peter, but excuse me if I don't join you in your choice. Unfortunately, my doctor has now forbidden me to eat anything except fillet steak.' My heart bled for him until I remembered that it was all on expenses anyway.

Talking of food another noteworthy event was the occasion when a commissioner invited the whole official committee on regional development to take lunch with him to celebrate something or other. Off we trooped to a nearby restaurant and sat down to a splendid meal in the course of which we noticed that all of us except the commissioner had the same menu but he had a large plateful of steak, chips and other vegetables. He must have seen that we had noticed the difference and stood up. 'Gentlemen, I must apologize that I do not eat the same food as you. But I have to confine myself to a light lunch because I am invited this evening to a formal dinner and must leave room to do it justice.' We spent some time after that surreptitiously debating the meaning of the words 'light' and 'heavy' as applied to Belgian meals.

Another food problem for British civil servants attending meetings in Brussels was how to find reasonably cheap restaurants where the prices bore some relationship to the fixed expense allowances sanctioned by the Treasury. Of course it is a long time ago now and everything may have changed, but we did find some good ones. For what it is worth two that stood us in good stead then were:

- *Chez Leon* — a fish restaurant just off the Grand Place. On scrubbed pine tables, it offered a superb range of fish dishes (with *moule*s in top place) all washed down with a very drinkable and reasonably priced Muscadet. A few years back they had done well enough to open a sister restaurant in Paris (near the Pompidou Centre). Suzanne and I did not find it as good as the Brussels one, but that may well be simple nostalgia.

- *Aux Armes de Bruxelles* — a conventional Belgian eatery for them as likes steak and chips. It is across the road from *Chez Leon* and good value for money (or at any rate it was good value in the old days). It is worth a try if it still exists.

I have one final food story. The Commission had a very exclusive dining room on the top floor of the Berlaymont where its offices were situated. The clientele was confined to commissioners, senior staff and their guests. One day, as we passed into this holy ground, an old-fashioned plummy English public school voice was heard to exclaim, 'Oh my God, not lobster again.'

And just to show that we did do some work, I recall a conversation with a nice Belgian director in which I sought to convince him that the British position on something or other was logical. 'That may well be so,' he said, 'the trouble is that there is more than one system of logic.'

This exchange came back to me when, a year or two later, I found myself in Paris at a European summit meeting where the PM and President Pompidou ('Pom Pom' to Parisian taxi drivers) were both present. Right at the beginning of the conference, as is the way of these things, officials of the countries concerned were wrestling with the wording of the final communiqué. John Hunt, who by this time was *en route* to being Cabinet secretary, came up with some very wise advice, which stood me in good stead in the years ahead — 'there is not much mileage to be got from disputing French logic. What you've got to do is to attack their premises.'

That meeting took place in the Hotel Kléber, named after an Alsatian hero of the French Revolution, and notorious as a building used by the Gestapo in Paris in the Second World War. The British and French delegations sat facing each other on opposite sides of a long narrow room with President Pompidou centre stage on one side and Edward Heath roughly centre stage on the other. The president, as was his habit, had a Gauloise cigarette dangling from his upper lip and spoke through a cloud of smoke. I am not sure after the lapse of over a quarter of a century whether the meeting achieved much. Most probably, like so many meetings of the kind, it was meant as a political demonstration rather than a proper negotiation. But at least we all parted as friends and our rather pathetic hopes of a fair share of a massive Regional Development Fund to offset the extravagances of the CAP were kept alive. The fund actually came into being in 1974 and, while useful, never came up to our expectations. But I suppose, from the point of view of the other member states, it helped to shut us up, temporarily at least, about the iniquities of the CAP and the monstrous injustice of the Common Fisheries Policy.

Beneath the Kléber was a labyrinth of rooms and passages that housed one of the canteens of the French foreign office, which the official delegates of both sides used to fuel up in the intervals between plenary sessions. As one might expect the food was very good and generated much Anglo–French chitchat. But, despite the bonhomie, the sinister history of the building and the rows of silent cellars imposed a dampener on the proceedings rather akin to those experienced at the site of a concentration camp or a notorious massacre by the SS like that at Oradour-sur-Glane. It was very creepy and difficult to reconcile with the close alliance that rules relationships today between France and Germany.

This solemn thought leads me to what I hope is a pertinent digression. It is often said that the origins of the EEC lie in the shared misery of a club of defeated nations. There may be something in this but I believe two other factors predominate. The first is a perceived failure of democracy in both France and Germany. The French certainly believe that their catastrophic defeat in 1940 is attributable to the stream of political nonentities of the United Front who tried and failed to rule France in the prewar years. It was in this period that the French intellectual meritocracy, which ran the civil service, had perforce to try and run the country as well. But far from implicating them in the disaster, this experience strengthened their belief that they were France's saviours and that defeat was the product of political infighting and incompetence interlaced with a strong dose of that classic French excuse for failure 'nous étions trahis' (we were betrayed).

I am less familiar with the German mindset on these matters but find it very easy to believe that, as in 1918, the German elite of 1945 also saw themselves as betrayed by the very low class hooligans of the Nazi party. After the most crushing defeat suffered by any nation for many centuries it must be very tempting to blame anyone but yourselves, particularly when you have been thoroughly soaked in the doctrines of intellectual and racial superiority. The essential point, however, is that the villains, as in France, were politicians.

It is my fancy that it is this mistrust of self-serving and incompetent politicians that led to the creation of an unelected and largely unaccountable Commission serviced and advised by an equally unaccountable corps of inflated intellectual egos. Of course not all the national players in this game are blind to the realities of Community management. General de Gaulle, for example, is credited with the authorship of the famous put-down '*La Commission? Ils sont des experts. Utile même.*' ('The Commission? They are experts. Sometimes even useful.')

Finally, for the French elite at least, there is a strong feeling of mortification that they have been saved twice in a generation by the uncouth and illiterate Anglo-Saxons. The ordinary people do not share this view but the elites of the Polytechnique and the École Nationale d'Administration were, one suspects, far from pleased that the great unwashed had triumphed yet again despite being, as one of the characters in Shakespeare's *Henry V* puts it, '[only] Norman bastards'.

Given the history it is hardly surprising that, from the outset, the Common Market has been a profoundly undemocratic organization run by an official elite in which the effective power of national politicians was severely limited by design at the outset and has been further eroded since. And, in all this, one of the saddest facts (well understood by the official elite) is that so many European politicians positively enjoy being raped. After all, the doctrine that the man in Brussels knows best offers a massive alibi and/or excuse for the cowards. Why think when some plausible Frenchman or German is willing to do it for you while putting on the flattery with a trowel? But to stay sane you must remember that his agenda is not yours but his own.

In the event, I moved on to another job before the Regional Development Fund became a reality, but it was fun getting the wagon rolling. I particularly enjoyed the slightly lunatic dance of the negotiations in which I wrote the negotiating brief in London and got authority for it. I then sent it to Brussels, rushed across the Channel to act on it, reported my progress by telegram to London and sought any new guidance that might be necessary, dashed home to process my telegram and send the necessary guidance to Brussels, and then went back there to implement my new orders. To adapt the words of the musical *Evita*, 'and the duty frees kept rolling in'.

23

Here We Go Again!

Towards the end of 1973 Egypt and Syria launched what came to be known as the Yom Kippur War on Israel and were rapidly joined by other oil producing countries in the Middle East. The price of oil soared and the economies of the Western world were thrown into turmoil. In this country the economic impact of the rise in the price of oil was heightened by a dispute with the coal miners over both wages and the government's incomes policy — that at least is what the history books tell us. But modern readers must remember that much of postwar political history in this country consists of a largely hidden battle for control of the Labour Party between the moderate majority and a Trotskyite minority who sought to seize power mainly through the constituency parties and the annual conference. This is not the place to examine this civil war in depth, but suffice it to say that, like most civil wars, it was prolonged, bitter and one of its first casualties was the truth. The recurring battles over incomes policy were part of this war.

Of course, this is all now old hat. The Soviet empire has collapsed; the ex-communist countries of eastern Europe have been exposed as hopelessly inefficient and among the greatest polluters of the environment that have ever existed; manual work is now largely banished from our society and with it the power of the mass unions; trade union power has also been much diminished by the reform of the law; and, as

Tony Blair has recently reminded us, the working class is now only a minority interest for politicians given that, by self definition, it is numerically overwhelmed by the middle class.

But, be all this as it may, the reality was of a country panicking over its energy supplies (to the extent of declaring a state of emergency in November 1973; and cutting the working week for industry generally to three days in December 1973). Moreover, in December the Shah of Persia announced the doubling of the price of crude oil. 'Oh dear,' someone must have said, 'not only have we abolished the Ministry of Power, which used to deal with these matters, but we have scattered its staff and the next general election is looming over the horizon. Reverse engines.'

And so the Department of Energy was born on 8 January 1974, its old Ministry of Power staff were dragged in from the four corners of the world and Peter Carrington was transferred from the Ministry of Defence to take charge of it. Not many people noticed that our new secretary of state brought his press officer from the ministry with him. His name was Bernard Ingham. Peter Carrington was not with us long enough to make his mark as secretary of state for energy but he impressed all of us who came in contact with him in that brief interlude. He was bright, hardworking and personally very pleasant and later became a distinguished secretary of state for defence in his second spell in the job. He is also the subject of a classic story. He fought in France after D-Day and had, as they used to say, a 'good' war. Of him it is alleged that his commanding officer wrote in his annual report — 'Young Carrington's men would follow him anywhere, if only out of curiosity.' There are worse judgements than that.

In the new department I was promoted to deputy secretary (the rank immediately below permanent secretary — a mandarin at last) and given wide ranging responsibilities for energy policy at home and abroad except for the exploitation of North Sea oil (which was regarded as a full-time charge for another deputy secretary) and the detailed supervision of the nationalized coal, gas and electricity industries, which was handled by yet another colleague. Among my specific topics were relations with the EEC (where I was our man on its official committee on energy policy) and the OECD (where I was our governor of the newly created International Energy Agency). I also looked after the divisions concerned with energy conservation and energy forecasting; it was helpful to me (but I suspect a pain for my troops) that I had served at one time or another in all of the divisions that now fell within my command.

Seven weeks after the re-creation of the energy department the general election was lost (just) by the Conservatives and Labour came to power as a minority government under the premiership of Mr Harold Wilson. Mr Eric Varley became secretary of state for energy. Bernard Ingham stayed on in the department as press officer.

The three-day week proved to be a surprisingly sturdy child with much lost output being replaced through higher productivity. At least we now knew what we could do if we tried.

The government's attempts to save energy by reducing heating standards gave the press a field day. We held press conferences almost every day and the press added thermometers to the journalists' do-it-yourself kit. This posed problems because, while we were well aware of the need for us (of all people) to keep to the law, fifty or so sweaty journalists generate a lot of body heat (roughly the heat output of three journalists equals that of a one bar electric fire). Consequently, ten minutes into a press conference and the mercury in the thermometers began to rise in an alarming way. We tried leaving windows open, but in mid-winter that sort of thing tends to get noticed. In the end the only thing we could do was to give the room a good airing before the mob arrived and hope that either they would cotton on to the simple science involved or get bored.

Incidentally, here is a tip for our successors if ever they have to cope with this sort of situation again. It is no longer enough to introduce a maximum permitted temperature in offices and shops to save fuel. As our American cousins found to their embarrassment, once air conditioning systems are in place it can take as much scarce energy to hold the temperature down to a given level as it does to hold it up to one.

Here is another tip. Ted Heath established the Central Policy Review Staff (CPRS) to give the government independent advice on policy issues. In the fuel crisis it was asked to consider and report on energy conservation. It did so and, as always, turned in a worthwhile report. But the really interesting comment (at any rate to a lateral thinker like me) came from Victor Rothschild (the then boss of the CPRS) when he said that really big savings in energy consumption (30 per cent of the national total) were available to any government with the courage to forget the law, ignore falling temperatures and give every member of the population a free set of thick woollen long johns. What a lovely idea!

Among other tried and trusted remedies we set up a very powerful advisory committee on energy conservation. Usually such committees are an excuse for inaction. (As Harold Wilson once remarked, committees of enquiry are devised to take minutes and waste years.) But this one was different because it succeeded in focusing the attention of top industrial management on a specific issue. One very compelling example came from the oil industry, which had for years regarded its refineries as very cheap parts of the chain between wellhead and petrol pump. Certainly the fuel they used was a waste product of the refining process with an opportunity cost of around zilch. But complacency about a very favourable fuel cost obscured the fact that refineries not only used fuel wastefully but also used a lot more people than they needed. Once a proper audit had been carried out costs fell dramatically.

Although we issued petrol coupons to our local offices we did not need to move to (or could not face the flak of moving to) petrol rationing as such. Rather, we relied on exhortation coupled with a massive advertising campaign. And thereby hangs a tale. As is government's wont, we hired expensive outside help to devise an advertising campaign for us. Unfortunately, when we got the results we did not like them very much. And so, very much as a last resort, a group of us were sitting round a table late at night tossing ideas back and forth and suddenly, from where I know not, the idea emerged of a rubber stamp crashing down on a piece of paper and leaving behind the imprint of 'SAVE IT'. Others

WHO SAYS THE CIVIL SERVICE CAN'T DO EVERYTHING FOR ITSELF?

may be able to pin down the genesis of this famous slogan more precisely than I can, but my memory is of the chorus of 'that's it', *'merde'*, 'shit', 'golly' and 'expletive deleted', which burst out from the whole company. It must have been like that the evening someone suggested 'Coca-Cola' as a brand name.

Who says the civil service can't do everything for itself if it tries?

It is an interesting commentary on the loosening up of civil service attitudes that when the crisis was over Bernard Ingham was converted into a mainstream undersecretary and given charge of our energy conservation division.

One outcome of the energy crisis was the creation, in 1974, of the International Energy Agency in Paris where it was attached for pay and rationing purposes to the OECD. The agency was a curious creature that set out to bind together the interests of the energy-using countries — though some of these (for example, the USA, UK and Norway) were also substantial oil producers in their own right. The imp in me wanted us all to apply to join OPEC, but most politicians and many civil servants are cowards at heart so we played by the old, dull rules. Be that as it may, the main operational task of the agency was to prepare to divide up equably the available oil supplies should OPEC again try to reduce, or stop, the sale of its oil to the developed world. In short, it was basically a technical mechanism. Politics and similar considerations were for others.

The one feature of the agency that was unusual was that the treaty that established it gave the power to activate its sharing mechanism to the official appointed to head the organization. He had, of course, to act within the framework laid down in the treaty but provided he did so the decision was his. This arrangement, which so far as I am aware is unique among international organizations, was never tested for real. But it made the agency stand out amid the toothless wonders of the OECD.

In due time I became chairman of the committee that devised and tested the sharing mechanism. This was a considerable technical challenge but it also brought me face to face with one of the most interesting facts of life when cohabiting internationally with the United States of America. This arises from the belief of the US Congress that it is entitled to supervise the activities of US bureaucrats, citizens and companies, wherever they may be, to ensure that they do not infringe US law (particularly anti-trust law) or the interests of their country. Thus, when my committee got under way we faced an early demand for members of the House of Representatives, or their research assistants, to sit in at our meetings. The reasoning behind this request was the firm belief of US politicians that if the representatives of two or more US oil companies meet together behind closed doors there will occur what Adam Smith described as 'a conspiracy against the public, or in some contrivance to raise prices'. The resulting conflict opposed two immovable forces. My committee saw no point in letting some US research student leak all our plans to OPEC; and the US oil companies saw no point in defying Congress and getting hammered by US anti-trust legislation. However, the diplomats earned their keep and squared the circle. How they did so we (wisely I think) never asked. All we cared about was that we had no strangers present. But with hindsight the UK should have adopted the US Constitution before joining the EU. What fun we could have had.

One true story about the agency is worth recording. Our chairman was a Belgian foreign office character of great charm and political toughness named Steve Davignon. One day a new member state joined us, and its ambassador rose to reply to a speech of welcome our chairman had made. He began by saying 'Mr Chairman, gentlemen, my government has asked me to read the following statement into the record.' 'Fine,' said Steve, 'just give it to the secretaries and they will make sure it is printed in our proceedings.' 'Oh no,' said the ambassador, 'I regret but my instructions are clear. I have been told to read it into the record and must do so.' 'OK,' said our chairman wearily (I think the actual words were '*vas-y mon vieux*'). So the ambassador began his task, Steve and the secretaries listened as politely as they could and the rest of us went off for a cup of coffee. No one ever refused a proffered short cut thereafter.

The day came when we had a grand rehearsal of our emergency arrangements. The representatives of the oil companies and the member states gathered together in a large room equipped with masses of communication gizmos and a monster map of the world. We started off with a picture of the real state of the world's oil transport system, with lots of little flags representing real tankers with information on their cargoes. Then there was an assumed pulling of the plug and a pause while the secretariat calculated everyone's oil entitlements at the assumed level of interruption (they had, of course, done this already to save time) and then the fun began — shades of Guiseppe's antics on the beach at Salerno with bidding proceeding to match physical supply to assumed demand. This was a very skilled process because, for example, oil refineries are choosy about the oil they can process, so the game was much more complicated than simply managing tonnage. Inevitably there were glitches (detecting which was, after all, the whole purpose of the exercise). Of course, these were early days and the whole thing became much more sophisticated later. But we made a good beginning.

It will be evident from the odd passage in this piece that I did not always see eye to eye with my colleagues from the Foreign and Commonwealth Office. But it goes without saying that most of them were personally charming and almost all were highly intelligent. Our occasional disputes were about policy and did not spill over into personal relationships. As proof of this I offer in evidence the time when the government embarked on a deliberate policy of temporarily exchanging staff between home departments and the FCO. In the course of this I acquired an FCO undersecretary to head my overseas team. Her name was Gill Brown and she later became only the second lady to be

appointed as one of HM ambassadors overseas (to the kingdom of Norway) where she was a great success. Her stint at
the Department of Energy was also a great success and I
enormously valued her friendship in the years that remained
to her.

In an earlier chapter I made mention of the pleasures of
travelling to Luxembourg in bad winter weather. But travel
to other weightier destinations could be just as frustrating.
At this time (and I do not think the practice has changed
since) the Brits tried to minimize the disruption of European
meetings to their normal work by travelling out to Paris or
Brussels early in the morning of the meeting or, when the
timings were against us, on the evening before. We then
came back to London in the evening when the meeting had
run its course. On the occasion I have in mind my aim was
to get to Paris after the close of business on the day before
the meeting, go to the meeting early on the following
morning and leave for home again when the meeting was
over. In the event, when I got to Heathrow I was told that
Paris was shut because of fog (shades of the old joke about
the Continent being isolated). After hanging around a short
while to see if matters improved (they did not) I did some
rapid telephoning and discovered that the back door to Paris
was still open. By this I mean the funny little airline that in
those days shuttled holidaymakers with cars to and from
Lydd to Le Touquet in boxy, and noisy, Bristol freighters.
Both airports were free of fog and if I rushed, they said, I
might just make the last one of the day. Once on the other
side I could get a train to Paris. So it was into a taxi and
pell-mell for Victoria station where there was an office
handling this traffic. On arrival, however, to my horror both
Lydd and Le Touquet were now fogbound. There was only
one thing left to do. In those days the British and French
railways ran an overnight rail ferry to Paris. This consisted
of some aged rolling stock, which rumbled slowly to Dover
where the railway coaches were pushed onto a specially

adapted ferry with railway tracks in the hold. Arriving at the other side of the Channel a French loco picked up the rolling stock and towed it by a roundabout route to Paris (I seem to remember that it went through Lille and you cannot get much more roundabout than that). Unlike the modern Euro trains, the objective of this train was not to arrive early at its destination on the grounds that its customers would not wish to be dumped in a Paris still washing its face. This was an objective the old-style BR and SNCF found suitably congenial. As for me, there was naturally no free berth so I sat up all the way. Nevertheless, I made it and, as the fog lifted during the day, I caught a plane back home that evening where I arrived tired but happy at having beaten the system.

24

Back to Jerusalem

Meanwhile, the general election of 1974 resulted in the return of a Labour government and the appointment of the nice, and very pragmatic, Eric Varley as secretary of state for energy. As it happens I had known Eric when he was a parliamentary private secretary to the prime minister during my stint at No 10, so we were not strangers. (It is an interesting, if little noticed, fact that junior ministers and officials grow up together.) At the same time Tony Benn (a.k.a. the Right Honourable Anthony Neil Wedgwood Benn to the history books and as 'Wedgie' or 'Wedgie Benn' to just about everyone else outside the ranks of the 'Yes Minister' circle) was appointed as secretary of state for industry. Eric Varley only remained with us for a brief spell before swapping jobs with Tony Benn in 1975.

The only point I would note about Eric's short term of office was that he became involved with the Labour government's plans for devolution and asked me to comment on a personal basis on some of the proposals being considered by ministers. I have, of course, no record of the comments I made but recall pointing out that devolution to some parts of the UK would not work unless England got equal treatment with Scotland, Wales and Northern Ireland, which in their turn would require equal treatment with each other (precisely as the *Lander* do under the German constitution). Also, the creation of a separate English parliament could, very easily, sound the death knell of the Labour Party as we had known it. The point at issue (also known as the 'West Lothian question' — see below) was not a novel one but is still (in the year of our Lord 2001) causing great difficulty for today's Labour government. The other fundamental issues that appear to stick in their throats are the logic of creating a legitimate (namely elected) second chamber as the ultimate guarantor against the potentially unbridled tyranny of an all-powerful House of Commons; and the inevitability of proportional representation for elections to the Commons leading to coalition government and the murky, not to say mucky, politics of the smoke filled room.

With hindsight I am still unable to think of any durable solution to the 'West Lothian question' beyond either following the German lead (by giving identical treatment to all the constituent parts of the federation), or excluding the Scottish, Welsh and Northern Irish MPs at Westminster from voting on any issue where power is devolved to their regional assemblies. Put crudely, why should such MPs vote on English topics where the English MPs cannot vote on the same issues in their home territories? But, of course, to divide Westminster's MPs into categories with differing voting rights would create a nightmare for the party managers in the Commons, especially when the government's majority was a slim one.

As to PR I would commend to the present government the Australian solution to the dilemma of combining the efficient governments stemming from 'first past the post' voting with the 'fair', but inefficient, system of PR. That solution is to elect the lower house in the traditional way and the upper house by some form of PR. Best of both worlds.

On returning to this subject, when the present government came to power in May 1997 I wrote a think piece entitled 'Devolution: Thirteen Questions for Democrats' and distributed it fairly widely. Only the Liberal-Democrats showed any interest and got so far as to ask me to comment on their constitutional proposals. I did so willingly only to find my views disappear into limbo, presumably because they were not congenial.

The basic trouble for all the political parties is that increasing democratic control inevitably means reducing the power of the party machines. For example, reducing the number of Westminster MPs by about half to bring us more into line with the USA would require us to shed about 300 of our present MPs. Now, not only would the MPs concerned find unemployment hard (although the population at large would no doubt welcome the saving of many millions of pounds from the parliamentary vote), but 300 chairmen of constituency parties would be redundant along with their attendant agents, treasurers, secretaries and committee members. One suspects that the courage to do anything of the kind will be on a par with that of turkeys asked to volunteer for Christmas.

The same sort of considerations will affect other aspects of constitutional change. For example, the last attempt at the reform of the House of Lords has left us with a legacy of about 500 life peers appointed by successive prime ministers. Only under the most undemocratic solution to the problem of devising a new second chamber can as many as 100 of them survive with a role in Parliament. What becomes of the others? Do we just let them die out? Do we strip them of their rank and have a grand bonfire of ermine? Perhaps we should do so on Guy Fawkes day. Do we take away from them the privilege of using the Lords as an exclusive club? If so do we pay compensation? And so on.

And, when it comes to PR, do we adopt the infamous list system where the party leader chooses the list from among his or her friends and cronies? And, whatever we do about that, should we not move closer to real democracy by adopting the device of primary elections where the people choose the party's candidates as well as the MP? In considering this, bear in mind that devolution will reinforce the tendency for the devolved assemblies to be one party states (60 per cent of our constituencies already are held by the same party for election after election and the geographical pattern of party loyalty will do the rest).

Of course we might move even closer to real democracy by adopting the device of referenda with the vote triggered by the electors. After all, the United States of America and Switzerland manage to live with direct democracy of this kind. Are the British really, as some of our politicians say privately, too thick to do the same? Or is it simply that the people's priorities and those of the politicians do not coincide? For example, if the people said 'hang convicted murderers' — as they almost certainly would — have our politicians got the guts to allow the execution of terrorists convicted of murder and accept the possible consequences for themselves?

There is a great deal of fun, not to say political capital, to be made out of these issues and the present opposition will be even more inept than it sometimes appears if it lets the chance pass it by. *Vas-y mes enfants!* And howl for answers when they try to duck. If the roles were reversed they would have your guts for garters. So there is no mercy. You have nothing to lose but perpetual opposition.

25

Through the Looking Glass

Following Tony Benn's appointment to energy I enjoyed several interesting, if sometimes frustrating, years of working with him. Up to that point I had thought of my years with Harold Wilson as being my post-graduate course in politics but life with Tony and his political advisers (Frances Morrell and Francis Cripps) added a few interesting extras. Several events stand out.

The first revolved around Tony's old fight for the control of government policy to be vested in the party's annual conference. This was the era when North Sea oil was beginning to come ashore in quantity and the conference passed a motion that said, in effect, that to provide employment, this oil should be refined in Britain rather than exported. Such a course was, of course, an economic nonsense. We had had from the 1940s onwards a refinery policy that aimed at providing the UK with sufficient refinery capacity to produce all the petroleum products we consumed. That was not in dispute. But the choice of crude to be refined was a question of chemical composition and price. North Sea crude was 'light', which meant that on distillation it yielded a larger proportion of higher priced products like motor spirit (petrol) than typical Middle Eastern crude oils, which contained a higher proportion of low value fuel oils, tars and bitumens. As it happened our consumption pattern was also weighted to the lower end of the barrel so that it made economic sense to sell a good proportion of our native crudes to others and feed our refineries with cheap and mucky crudes from the Middle East. But Tony was never going to accept arguments, however strong, that showed the conference to be fallible. And I was my usual stubborn self when I thought that right was on my side. In the event the argument petered out. Tony demonstrated that he could sustain an argument, whether good, bad or indifferent, forever if he chose; and I came to realize that the argument was about politics not truth and that what mattered was that we had no powers to enforce Tony's view and precious little chance of getting them from his colleagues. So why bother?

Incidentally, I am quite unable to answer the question of why successive Labour prime ministers put up with Tony Benn if only because no one ever confided the answer to me. The most plausible, and it must be confessed the dullest of a range of possible answers is that, as all political parties are coalitions, each major faction must be given some representation in the Cabinet if it is to be kept onside. Of course, being careful men, prime ministers also took the precaution of providing Tony with ministerial seconds in command from the right of the party. Two notable examples were John Smith and Dr Dickson Mabon. The latter also gained undying fame in the department by telling Tony Benn (forever armed with an electric kettle and a large mug) that excessive tea drinking was bad for his health.

Other events illustrate the more exciting side of working with our new minister. The first was when, in 1977, the UK found itself coming to the top of the rota and thus holding the 'presidency' of the EEC for six months. This meant that UK ministers took the chair of the Council of Ministers in its various guises (Tony, for example, became chairman of the Energy Council). At the same time I became chairman on the official energy committee (made up of senior energy officials from each member state), which handled ongoing business and serviced the ministerial council.

At a very early stage my minister set off to visit his counterparts in the other member countries and his private secretary and I went with him. The visits all followed the same pattern, a friendly welcome, generous hospitality and a wide-ranging (if inconclusive) discussion of current energy issues. So far, so conventional, but then the talks changed gear as Tony opened up on his favourite subject — the lack of openness in the decision making processes of the Community. Why not, argued he, publish the papers being considered by the Commission and the Council of Ministers? And why not let the press and the public sit in on council meetings? The reaction was always the same: shock, horror and wriggle wriggle. Politeness struggled with incredulity as a master logician pressed the case. At least one minister blushed (he was an ex-journalist theoretically wedded to open government) but none succumbed. After all they, like their British counterparts, had no desire to commit political suicide.

In the light of subsequent history it is clear that Tony Benn had right on his side. The trouble was that all the European ministers thought, inevitably perhaps, in terms of their national government experience and brought their habits of mind with them to Brussels. Even that far back the battle lines were being set in an attempt to create a framework for a supranational state — and for that very surreptitious exercise the worst national techniques of secrecy and news management were brought into play. Let the press in? You must be joking!

As an interesting example of the importance of words, the tactics of the pro-federalists are worth studying. To call the European Economic Community the European Union was to convince many people that the process of integration had gone much further forward than was in fact the case. And, of course *faits accomplis* have a momentum of their own. Another example is the use of the word 'president' to describe the leading figure in the Commission. To the Anglo-

Saxon mind, and no doubt to others, the word equates the holder of this office with the president of, say, the USA or France. This is not so. In this context it means no more than 'chairman'. Unfortunately, the French language is deficient in providing only one word for two very different functions, so chairman will not do. Moreover, given that the members of the Commission are appointed, not elected, the most appropriate translation is probably 'chief commissioner'. Of course, if we wanted to deflate the egos of over mighty subjects we could propose 'chief clerk' (which is, of course, an honourable job description of a very senior official in the Foreign Office). Now, that would put the cat among the pigeons.

TO HIS CREDIT TONY SAID 'GO'

Oh yes! It is back to basics. One of our earliest European tours took us from Northolt to Luxembourg in an executive jet picked up by HMG from a bankrupt company that owed it a lot of money. When we got to Northolt the weather was foul. The pilot regarded Tony with a quizzical look in his eye and said 'Minister, you were a pilot once and must have flown in worse weather than this. I think we can make it safely, although the ride could be a bit bumpy. Do you want to go now, or should we wait a few hours in the hopes of better weather?' To his credit Tony said 'go'. So we went bumping along through rainstorms and poor visibility, which lasted until the treetops of the Ardennes appeared through the murk followed swiftly by a very close look at Luxembourg airport. I, for one, was grateful that it had been built large enough to handle B-52s.

One other memory of that tour is worth a mention. The British embassy in The Hague is located in a very fine old house constructed many centuries ago. Among other things this house enjoys the privilege of a private ghost. 'So what,' you may say, 'a ghost is normal in a building of that age.' But this one is different because the building was changed internally at some stage by the insertion of an extra floor. However, the ghost takes no notice of events since its death and, in consequence, walks on the floors of the house as they were in its day. This has the alarming result that the ghost is visible in two modes — either as legs and feet strolling under the ceiling or as the upper half of a body gliding across the floor. I did not see it myself but am quite prepared to accept that in a house that old anything can happen.

The next vignette is more tragic. Tony was invited in his capacity of secretary of state to visit the Shah of Persia and went to Tehran accompanied by Frances Morrell, his private secretary and me. Six things stand out in my memory. For light relief, there was the traffic in Tehran driving relentlessly both ways down the centre of the road. Also funny were the fairly frequent power cuts that led to Frances and me being trapped in the hotel lift. Luckily, the rescuers were well practised. The third was the staggering opulence of the audience room in the Shah's palace. Everything in that room was made of gold or crystal and glittered. Moreover, the effects were magnified by seemingly endless mirrors and electric lights. The Shah must have had a stand-by generator somewhere around so that the show did not get switched off by the erratic behaviour of the public electricity supply.

The fourth was the story told to us by diplomats from another embassy than our own about a visiting businessman who was totally unfamiliar with the protocol of talking to the Shah. The embassy accordingly drilled him in how to comport himself and in the course of this mentioned that the Shah occupied the 'peacock throne' of ancient Persia. Came zero hour and the flustered businessman bowed to the Shah and uttered the immortal words, 'how do you do, your Peacock Majesty.'

Next, Tony and the Shah talked to each other with no apparent comprehension on either side and Tony engaged in a considerable amount of circumlocution in an attempt to avoid uttering the dread words 'Your Imperial Majesty'.

And, finally, the meeting with the Iranian prime minister and some of his colleagues when the talk got round, as it tended to do in those days, to the activities of the CIA in the region. The punch line came when the Iranian PM said with admiration in his voice, 'After all, they are not schoolboys you know.' Little did we guess that the revolution was looming and that many of those at that meeting would die in the course of it.

But, however tempting it may be, I must not let Tony Benn dominate my narrative. One interesting development during this period was that we reached an agreement with the French government under which we had a bilateral exchange of views with them every six months about energy issues. Thus every six months either I went to Paris or my French opposite number came to London. The usefulness of these exchanges lay, not in concrete achievements, but in the insight they gave us into each other's manner of thought.

Three moments have stuck in my mind. The first illustrates, through a minor incident, the discreet manner in which our French colleagues exercise power. Phillipe, as I will call my French counterpart, gave me a lift to a meeting in his official car. As we were driven through central Paris I noticed that the policemen at road junctions gave us priority of passage. Given that our car was a standard black Citröen I thought it very clever of them to identify us from among dozens of similar vehicles. Then I twigged the trick. High on the windscreen behind the interior mirror was a small red, white and blue rosette. When we approached a junction with a policeman attached the driver pressed a button. The rosette lit up. And the policeman waved us through. *Simple, n'est ce pas?*

The second illuminating event came in a conversation I had with one of Phillipe's staff when I remarked that Phillipe was a very intelligent man. 'True,' said his aide, 'and do you realize that he actually comes from Nancy?' These words, in print, do not convey the full meaning. But the tone of voice made it quite clear that a high intelligence was not normally to be expected from inhabitants of that town in northeast France or indeed from anywhere else outside the holy ground of Paris. I had, quite inadvertently, stumbled upon one of the main fissures in French public life — the deep divide that separates Paris from the provinces. The origins of this divide lie buried in history. In medieval times 'France' meant the 'Isle de France', which had the town of Paris at its heart. This 'France' was a small country surrounded by independent neighbours. As the years passed France expanded to embrace its present territories while Paris remained as the centre of government and the home of the king and his court. There is a sense therefore in which the relationship between the centre and the periphery of France is akin to that of a metropolitan power and its colonies.

The division between the two became manifest with the revolution when the Paris mob set out with fierce cruelty to bring the provinces to the true faith — much as Trotsky and the Red Army did in Russia 150 years later. The resulting wounds did not heal. And then the lost war of 1870 destroyed both the national army and central authority and, in doing so, opened the door to the revolutionary seizure of Paris and the establishment of the Paris 'Commune' — an act rapidly followed by the bloody destruction of the Commune when the tattered armies of the provinces took their revenge under the fascinated gaze of a German army ostentatiously sitting on its hands. And so on through the resumed cultural and political domination of a purged Paris as the centre of France dictated manners and morals not only to France but also to its growing overseas empire. But the scars ran deep. Even as recently as 1940, when my wife's father, retreating with the rest of the French army through the south, was greeted by locals calling down hell and damnation on *'vous et votre guerre du nord'*. The English sometimes say in jest that the frozen north begins at Watford. The Parisians are quite certain that outer darkness begins at the *périphérique*.

The other illuminating insight I had into French thinking came one day when I commiserated with Phillipe on France's lack of success in finding oil off the French coast. 'That is why,' he said, 'we are putting so much effort into developing nuclear power.' And today, with 60 per cent of France's electricity generated by nuclear plant, and much of the rest from hydroelectric schemes, France has a valuable resource of cheap electricity, which we have largely denied ourselves. Of course, with the French being a nation of high-class engineers, their nuclear power is safe, but we too are blessed with safety conscious engineers of quality. The difference lies in the national ability to look reality in the face. Remember 1940 when the Brits kept on fighting against all reason whereas the French, quite logically, gave in? This trait served us well then, but reinforced by scientifically illiterate journalists and frightened politicians, sometimes serves us ill.

There is much about modern life that I welcome with open arms. But one of my strongest complaints is that, no doubt as a result of our less than perfect educational system, we appear to have totally lost the power to judge relative risks. To take a few examples — in the field of nuclear power it is safer to sit on top of a nuclear reactor than in an Aberdeen house built, as most are, of radioactive granite; if the thought of combat knives keeps you awake at night remember that any serviceman (and most servicewomen) of my vintage will tell you that one of the best emergency weapons in close quarter combat is a simple screwdriver; if T-bone steak is your *bête noire* ask the pundits to tell you the mathematical odds of it killing you other than through obesity; genetically modified food has not, so far as I know, killed anyone yet; the destruction of licensed hand guns was both expensive and daft since most guns used by criminals are unlicensed; and so on. The plain fact is that we (or more accurately politicians and journalists allegedly acting on our behalf) panic in a manner to put Corporal Jones of *Dad's Army* to shame. It seems to me that 'we the people' are entitled to ask the government and media to accompany every scare story with a mathematical assessment of the extent of the risk so that we can balance it against the cost. It is a salutary fact that the number of suspected deaths from BSE is substantially smaller than the number (around 50) recorded each year of people drowned in their bath. Surely when this is widely appreciated our lords and masters should not only ban bathing but should rip all of these dangerous baths from our homes (paying compensation of course) so as to remove temptation from our path. The only obstacles I can see is that small boys do not vote and fastidious modern females dislike smells.

Our French neighbours, on the other hand, are realists whose approach is well illustrated by a remark made by my French brother-in-law when we chided his countrymen for cutting down a pretty forest by the Rhine to make way for an industrial estate. 'It would,' said Joe, 'bring in money and jobs and, in any case, there is still a lot of scenery left'. It is also relevant that the French approach to industrial development is user-friendly. It is not too much of a parody to say that, when the French government wants to build a nuclear power station, it pays generous amounts of money to those immediately affected, and arranges for interfering outsiders, seeking to deprive good French *citoyens* and *citoyennes* of their financial due, to be hit on the head by the gentlemen of the *Corps républicain de securité*. Who are the pragmatists now?

This thought brings me, relatively easily, to a problem that, although here illustrated by a reference to Tony Benn, is to be found in most ministers of most political parties. I refer to the forecasting of future events. One day Tony asked me for a forecast of the demand for British coal in 25 years time. I got the lads to crank the handle of our mighty Wurlitzer (for the uninitiated the name given to a breed of very large and complex cinema organs in the days when a visit to the grander cinemas was an adventure and that was applied by extension to any large piece of machinery). In due course, the answer came forth from our splendid mathematical model. It was that in 25 years time there was a 90 per cent probability that demand for British coal would lie between 50 and 150 million tons. When presented with this, our minister's reaction was that such a forecast, however accurate, was of no use to him. Surely we could narrow the forecast down to a number on which policy could be based? We could not do so. The problem from which so many politicians shy away is that of uncertainty. As Mr Harold Macmillan once said in relation to short-term economic forecasts, 'they involve looking up next year's trains in last year's Bradshaw' and no amount of wishing will make it otherwise.

The real trouble is that politicians loathe admitting that they are not omnipotent while forecasts are, by their very nature, uncertain. Most businessmen know this and spend a good deal of time trying to limit their risks. Usually, of course, it is the gamblers who make a fortune or go bankrupt but at least most of them are risking some of their own money. Unfortunately, the number of politicians who are prepared to admit to ignorance is limited — although that number includes some of the best. It was after all Sir Winston Churchill who memorably answered a supplementary question aimed at showing his ignorance of the detail on a particular subject by saying, 'I am flattered that the Right Honourable gentleman should think I keep that sort of information in my head.' But, of course, as Robert Louis Stevenson remarked in the 1880s, 'Politics is perhaps the only profession for which no preparation is thought necessary.' And, if you doubt the adverse results of this go and listen to the prattling of the backbench members of all parties in the House during the dead hours of the late afternoon and the early evening. For these are the hours when the stars who have opened the debate in good time for the six o'clock news bulletins are relaxing in Annie's Bar; and the late evening 'winders up' are still polishing their words for tomorrow morning's newspapers.

This outburst enables me to pontificate about the failings of Whitehall/Westminster (indissolubly linked as they are like Sinn Fein/IRA). Looked at in the round there are three principal sins of omission or commission. The first, as noted above, is the unwillingness of most politicians to admit to error or to changing their views. A good example was the immense reluctance of many Labour activists to admit that clause four of the party's constitution (which set the party's goal as being to bring all the means of production, distribution and exchange into public ownership) was incompatible with a free society and thus was a political gift of great value to the Conservative Party.

The second is the habit of British administrations to reinvent the wheel whenever faced with a practical problem.

The origins of this extremely wasteful practice lie in part in the institutional make-up and habits of the Whitehall machine. For example, both ministers and officials are moved between jobs very frequently so that there is very little continuity of experience (even less of shared experience) among those involved. In addition, valiant attempts to create an internal history recording experience of the handling of major policy issues (known when first formulated as the 'funding of experience') have died through over-zealous cost cutting. Thus, every time there was a need for a new incomes policy, or anything of that kind, there was a mad scratching through files to see what we did last time.

The third is the result of our adversarial form of political infighting. In reality, external forces drive 80 per cent of government decisions. Madmen invade their neighbours; a major world economy collapses; a revolution occurs; scientists frighten; newspapers exaggerate; politicians play politics; and so on. I illustrated the yo-yo effect of politics on the fortunes of the steel industry earlier in this book. Anyone seeking a more homely proof of this phenomenon need only glance at any OAP's letter from the DSS setting out how his or her pension is made up — lots of little bits from lots of discontinued bright ideas of pension reform.

26

To Them That Hath Shall Be Given

I t was in this period, too, that I found myself leading an EEC team at the Conference on International Economic Cooperation (CIEC) in Paris and that I nearly joined the staff of the Commission in Brussels. Both events have lessons to teach that are worth recording.

To take the CIEC first, the issue of international aid has troubled the world community for many years. There are those in the West who genuinely feel compassion for their less well off brethren overseas and whose efforts are mainly concentrated through the voluntary aid charities. They were, and are, the twentieth century's saints. There are those too who have bad consciences about our colonial past, though the number with direct experience of the subject has never been large. Throughout the period there have been politically incorrect realists who have maintained that the ex-colonial states' real problems in the latter part of the twentieth century are due to the greed and incompetence of their new masters. In addition, at the time of which I speak, the cold war raged and the communist propaganda mills worked overtime on those in the West Lenin had earlier classified as 'useful fools' or who, in the terminology of the American right, were known as 'bleeding hearts'. There were also countries that recognized that international aid, properly directed, was a useful source of business for their own economies and a useful source of power for their foreign policies. The French, realistic to the last, were prominent among the latter group and, in effect, adopted the old Yorkshire motto, 'If ever tha' does out for nowt, allus do it for thissen!'

The basic arguments had rumbled on for years but had changed with fashion. In the 1970s the broad outline of the row between haves and have-nots had crystallized in tabloid speak as the 'North–South divide' and the sovereign remedy of the day as the 'transfer of technology'. The trouble in the late 1970s was that the pressure of high oil prices was savaging most economies without oil of their own, and the clamour for relief had become a political force in its own right. Unfortunately, the North–South divide was not the problem. The real divide was between those with and those without oil. Unfortunately, too, a political realignment to reflect this was not on. In consequence, the UN, faced with yet another profitless wrangle on these matters, chose the easy way out by setting up a new international conference. It was given the high-sounding label of the Conference on International Cooperation and convened in Paris for about six months to the joy of the French leisure industry and the delight of the potential delegates from the more puritanical regimes in the Middle East. The UN secretariat knew its business.

The European Commission had to be in on the act and, because of the importance of oil to the issues, my official committee on energy was given a prominent role in the ranks of the wicked northerners. Came the day and we all (including the ghosts of the Gestapo and its victims) foregathered once more at the French government's conference centre in the Avenue Kléber.

The proceedings were as tedious as expected — day after day of hot air with much smoke but little light. Such fun as there was came from teasing the other side in the corridors with questions like, 'What do you mean by the transfer of technology? Do you want teachers or for us to buy patents and hand them over free? If the latter which kinds of patents and who will get them?' In any case we would point out very gently (I say very gently because politically correct Western politicians might object to the questions being asked in their names) that the 'South' for the purposes of UN rhetoric included the oil-rich states of the Middle East, which had as much need of handouts as our combined left feet, and were rich enough to buy anything they pleased and give it to anyone they pleased.

It was also the case, we hinted, that what we were all really talking about was investment in underdeveloped countries by Western companies and that the real obstacles to such investment lay in the lack of effective legal protection for investors in many poor countries and the existence of widespread corruption in most of them. None of this was said openly, of course, because telling the truth is not encouraged in diplomatic circles although everyone present knew it perfectly well. Indeed, the realities of the conference could be seen every evening when the delegates from Western countries walked or took the Métro back to their hotels and the delegates from 'poor' countries climbed into their chauffeur driven Mercs and headed, presumably, for the fleshpots. As the bittersweet definition of 'overseas aid' current among Western civil servants had it, such aid was 'money taken from the poor in rich countries and given to the rich in poor countries'. There were also those among us who, while wholly sold on the need for humanitarian aid, felt that the most useful economic aid would be a cargo or two of Samuel Smiles's Victorian tract *Self-Help* or, as the late twentieth century would express it, 'how to pull yourselves up by your own bootstraps'.

But the whole thing was really play-acting and a dreadful waste of time and money. It says a lot for the seriousness with which our 'developing' friends viewed the conference that, at its end, a number of the key delegates did not stay around to contribute to the, admittedly flaccid, final communiqué.

The other event was my almost departure to take the post as director general of the energy directorate of the EEC in Brussels. The post fell vacant in 1976 and, for some reason best known to the denizens of Brussels, it was made known that a UK candidate would be welcome. I was then approached and asked to let my name go forward. It was hinted, too, that as a well-known figure on the international energy scene and with a French wife, my chances of success were good. The offer of such a job was very tempting and a brief study of the EEC staff rules showed that it would be very rewarding as well. There were, however, snags. At the age of 50 and as a deputy secretary of three years seniority and wide experience, I had, I thought, a good chance of making permanent secretary if I stayed at home. The money in Brussels was better, but the degree of power and freedom would be a good deal less. Other reasons also pressed. My eldest son was coming up to his O levels and the other two were not far behind. It would, my wife and I thought, be wrong to pull them from school at this particular period of their schooling and project them into a totally strange environment with different syllabuses, a different culture and a language that they knew in part but whose scholastic vocabulary would be largely unknown to them. But if they stayed behind so, inevitably, would Suzanne. Of course I could commute at weekends, but even this would be difficult given the paucity of the transport links of the day and the amount of travelling otherwise involved in the energy job. The truth is we were a very close-knit family and neither of us relished the thought of the sort of life to which we would be committing ourselves. In short, the opportunity in Brussels came either three years too soon or three years too late for us to take it on. So I turned the chance down and a colleague, Leonard Williams, went in my stead. As it happened, the opportunity recurred some four years later and this time I said 'yes' and Brussels said 'no'. I will deal with the interesting circumstances of this rebuff in a later chapter.

Before moving on to the next big event in my life it may be useful to my readers if I impart a little of the flavour of the pay system of the Community as it was then and as it almost certainly still is. The starting point is that the pay system is embodied in a legally binding document of great complexity. Change is very difficult and any disputes about meaning are the province of the European Court. Add to this the fact that the original agreements were drawn up by the staff's legal advisers on the one hand and the Council of Foreign Ministers on the other and it is not surprising that the whole document is heavily weighted in favour of the troops.

Philosophically, the framework is set by the manner in which Napoleon paid his conscript armies, the practices of Europe's diplomatic services and the extension of such practices to the various international organizations that have proliferated since the Second World War.

The link with Napoleon's army is clear. The cost of a large army is formidable. Luckily, the unmarried conscripts in an army need be paid no more than pocket money. Soldiers with family responsibilities, however, need more if their families are to be sustained and their loyalty retained — hence special allowances for wives and children. The pay structures of civil services whose origins lie in Napoleonic France follow the same pattern. Basic pay scales are topped up with allowances relating to family circumstances — so much extra for the 'head of a family', so much more for each child and so on. As a cynic might put it, pay in the French civil service does not reflect the value of work to the employer but the sexual prowess of the individual concerned.

Add to this the practices of the diplomatic services of Europe: tax free pay, the provision of duty free goods, lucrative educational allowances and special pay supplements to offset the cost of working abroad. Call in aid, too, the extension of these practices to the employees of international bodies like the various agencies of the UN to which the Eurocrats can point as an excuse for parallel treatment, and the scene is set for an almighty rip-off. Of course, some concessions have been made to public opinion, notably by the levying of a token level of income tax, but the reality remains of snouts firmly embedded in a deep trough.

If European governments want to tone down the enthusiasm of Brussels for a unitary super state they should insist that the present degree of integration justifies moving to a similar pay regime to that of the USA — pay related to work done; no special allowances; no freedom from the full rigour of local taxation; and an unrewarded mobility obligation within the territory of the European Union. For some at least such a regime would rekindle General de Gaulle's vision of a '*Europe des patries*'.

But so much for the might-have-beens, I had made my decision and I stuck to it. Moreover, the wheel soon span again and less than two years later I was offered the job of head of the economic and scientific secretariat in the Cabinet Office. I accepted without any hesitation and began work in that, by now very familiar building, at the beginning of January 1978.

27

The Heart of the Matter

A t the turn of the year 1977/8 I was rung up by John Hunt and told that a vacancy had unexpectedly occurred for the post of head of the economic secretariat. Was I interested? 'Yes please,' I said enthusiastically. Within days I had moved back into that familiar building in Whitehall. I remained there for nearly three and a half years. For the first year and a quarter of this period I watched the then Labour Party and government commit suicide. For the next two years and a bit I watched the Thatcherite revolution plough up much of the old political, economic and cultural landscape of this country and sow it with new plants. But before I launch into an account of these stirring times I must once more beg the indulgence of my readers as I divert into the thinking that underlay our actions and determined the way we worked.

In essence, the secretariat was ruled by the legacies of the brilliant men who had led and moulded it over the decades since 1916. At that time Maurice Hankey, acting in concert with and at the direction of David Lloyd George, built a structure that endures, in its essentials, to this day. The efforts of Edward Bridges during the Second World War consolidated the secretariat's reputation as a Rolls-Royce machine. And the postwar regimes of Norman Brook, Burke Trend, John Hunt and Robert Armstrong brought it safely through successive periods of great change in our national fortunes. Norman Brook's achievements in codifying the work of the secretariat made a particularly notable contribution to maintaining its basic ethos and thus to ensuring its continued acceptance by both Whitehall and Westminster as impartial and trustworthy.

It is worth noting at the outset that the doctrine of 'collective responsibility', which rules the political life of British governments, is not simply a device to justify the imposition of party discipline but is the vital cement that binds an administration together. As Benjamin Franklin remarked at the signing of the American Declaration of Independence in 1776, 'We must indeed all hang together, or most assuredly we shall all hang separately.' It is interesting too that Stalinist Russia had the same doctrine (which Uncle Joe labelled 'democratic centralism') although the methods of enforcement were different.

Given our system of parliamentary democracy the doctrine of 'collective responsibility' has a powerful impact on the work of the Cabinet secretariat. In particular, the fact that getting on for one hundred sitting members of the House of Commons (the so-called 'payroll vote') plus about twenty members of the House of Lords are appointed to be ministers or party officials in Parliament (the so-called 'whips' who maintain party discipline) poses a real problem of accountability. For junior ministers and whips, information about policy formation can be restricted on a need to know basis, but if senior ministers are to be held accountable for the decisions of government, they must have access to good and timely information on what the government decides and why.

The Cabinet secretariat provides this facility through the form and handling of its main output — the record of the proceedings of the ministerial committees it services. It was Norman Brook's legacy to his succeeding scribes to codify the form taken by the records of the meetings of ministerial and official committees held under the aegis of the Cabinet

Office. Essentially, such minutes fall into three parts. They begin with a description of the issue to be discussed and of the papers before the committee. They end with a statement by the chairman describing the decision of the committee, together with instructions as to who does what, by when, to implement it. And, in between, lies a brief résumé of the main points made in the discussion.

To avoid subsequent bickering over words, the only statements normally attributed to individuals are the explanatory words of the person introducing the subject (adapted, if necessary, by the secretaries to give a self-contained picture of the issues and the papers before the committee) and the chairman's summing up. The 'points made in discussion' are not, except in very exceptional circumstances, attributed to individuals. The objective of this form of construction is that the resulting text gives those reading it who were not present, a self-contained record of the issues, the main arguments, the conclusion reached and of the action to be taken by whom and by when. Any minister receiving the minutes can, therefore, be assumed to be *au fait* with what is going on in the committee concerned.

There is, of course, more to the minuting process than getting the words right. As anyone involved in governing any institution by committee will be aware, sloth or malice can, in the old army phrase, 'baffle brains'. And one of the simplest ways of doing this is to delay the circulation of the minutes of a meeting until the participants have either forgotten what happened or no longer care. The creators of the Cabinet secretariat were well aware of all the ploys and laid it down from the outset that minutes of ministerial meetings should be circulated within 24 hours of the end of the meeting concerned and that Cabinet 'conclusions' should be available on ministers' desks first thing on the morning following the meeting no matter at what late hour the meeting terminated. This speed of circulation means that the minutes of any committee serviced by the Cabinet secretariat can be, and are, not simply a record for history — or if needs be for a later postmortem — but double as Whitehall's operating instructions. It is a strong tribute to Whitehall's trust in the secretariat that, when really urgent matters are being decided, departments will accept a hurried phone call from a sometimes quite junior committee secretary as their marching orders without waiting for the minutes to be circulated. It should be noted, too, that departmental trust is enhanced by the knowledge that in almost all ordinary circumstances the secretaries deliberately do not clear the minutes with the chairman of the committee concerned.

One last point needs to be made on the question of the form of the minutes. The British system has the (to us) great merit that it not only buttresses collective responsibility but that it serves to explain to senior officials the reasoning behind the decisions taken by both ministers and officials. In this it is at the opposite pole from the common form of recording to be found in most non-democratic societies. As we now know from the ex-communist countries, explanation was regarded as dangerous. Not only did it invite the attention of the KGB or its local equivalent, it also spread knowledge (that dangerous commodity) beyond the bounds of those who positively needed to know what was going on. In post-Soviet years I was privileged to be present at a meeting of the Cabinet of a newly free eastern European country and watched the old techniques at work. The minutes were confined essentially to a record of the decisions taken and their distribution was very limited. The dissemination of 'atmosphere' was achieved by allowing a few trusted senior civil servants to listen from the sidelines — though mostly, I suspect, they kept their inner knowledge strictly to themselves when they got back to their desks. After all, knowledge is power and it imparts a strong boost to the ego.

Minimalist reporting of this kind inevitably gives a distorted picture of what is going on when the various eyewitness accounts are filtered back to base. Indeed, as a student of British constitutional history, I was reminded of a meeting of the British Cabinet held in 1841 long before any secretarial help was available to provide an authoritative description of events. As this meeting was breaking up Lord Melbourne, the prime minister of the day, called the departing ministers back and asked, 'What did we decide? Is it to lower the price of bread or isn't it? It doesn't matter which, but we must all say the same thing.' Or, to put it another way, the passing of oral accounts from hand to hand (I mean of course from mouth to mouth) risks the distortion beloved of Cubs and Brownies when they play a game based on the First World War joke of the message passed down the trench from soldier to soldier. In the story the message started life as 'send reinforcements, I'm going to advance' and ended up as 'send three and four pence I'm going to a dance'. No wonder the Soviet empire was so inefficient.

28

Those Whom the Gods Wish to Destroy

When I moved into the Cabinet Office at the beginning of 1978 the Labour government was in dire straights. With its parliamentary majority dependent on a pact with the Liberals the party was wracked by internal disputes at constituency and local government level in which the antics of the Trotskyite Militant Tendency loomed large. Add to this a trade union movement seemingly bent on committing suicide and the Labour government's chances of survival seemed thin. Inevitably, politics bedevilled policy at every turn and, odd as it may seem, the Cabinet Office offered an oasis of rationality in a mad world. Our job, as always, was to facilitate decision taking in as efficient a manner as the situation allowed. But we were the engine room, not the bridge. Steering the ship was the sole responsibility of our elected masters and neither they nor we ever forgot it.

The full history of the death of 'this great movement of ours' in its socialist incarnation cannot be written until the Cabinet's books are opened in 2008/9 or the government finds the courage to pass a meaningful Freedom of Information Act. Incidentally, the enemies of free access to government information are not, as is often alleged, the civil servants but the politicians. In my experience, and apart from sensitive information about individuals or commercially valuable secrets, only politicians have anything to fear from freedom because it would inevitably expose the working of their minds and lead to questions about their competence. Frankly, asking ministers to come clean about the real reasons for their decisions is to require a triumph of hope over experience.

Given the paucity of real public information bearing on these events (including the thinness of the relevant ministerial memoirs) I cannot write much more than banalities here. But at least I can set the scene. The real question that exercised the Labour government in 1978 was how to stay alive until their electoral prospects improved enough to give some hope of winning the next election, the last possible date for which was in the summer of 1979. As matters stood at the outset of 1978 the omens were not good. As already noted, the government was sustained in power by a pact with the Liberal Party (a pact that collapsed later in the year); inflation was still seen as the overwhelming economic problem and, for the Labour Party at least, a voluntary incomes policy was the only politically acceptable means of combating it. This is not the place to attempt an account of the troubled postwar history of anti-inflation policy and the role of pay policy within it. But suffice it to say that the Labour movement was split three ways on the issue. The fault lines were inevitably political ones. On the right stood the conventional politicians led by Prime Minister Jim Callaghan, who believed that success in fighting inflation was the key to victory at the polls. In 1978 they pushed through the 5 per cent pay norm, which the government adopted in the autumn as the foundation of a new drive for economic recovery. In addition, many in this group argued for delaying the election until well into 1979 to give the economic policies time to work. On the left stood the small, but highly organized and vocal group of Trotskyists who adopted the *nom de guerre* of the Militant Tendency to

THE RT. HON. LORD CALLAGHAN OF CARDIFF, KG, PRIME MINISTER 1976–79

survive within the Labour Party (although far from funny as individuals or as a group, the Trots irresistibly reminded me of the Ronald Searle cartoon showing a hostess introducing a newcomer to a drinks party. The new guest was a spotty young man dressed in a pullover and baggy corduroys. The caption read 'THIS IS MR SO-AND-SO. HE WANTS A BLOODY REVOLUTION, YOU KNOW'). This, of course was also the aim of the Militants who saw the fomentation of chaos and confusion as the first step to power. In their view those who followed the line of making capitalism work were class traitors, fit only for some future Gulag. The third players were the trade unions whose leaders were not only doubtful about the Labour Party's chances in the next election, whenever called, but also were frightened to death by the reforming zeal of the new Thatcherite Conservative Party. In this situation a cynic might assume that their aim was the simple one of grabbing whatever they could for their members before the roof fell in. Whatever the motivation (and I claim no special knowledge) the plain fact is that the 'winter of discontent' was a disaster for the Labour movement. It is, of course, a fading memory now. No one under the age of 35 had left school when it happened, the media choose to ignore it and even the Tory Party fails to exploit it. This is a great pity because, politics apart, the events of the winter of 1978/9 were highly dramatic and have left a legacy of film and sound recordings that should make any TV or radio producer slobber in his beer.

Think of it, a government fighting for its life, violence foreshadowing that of the miners' strike of the early 1980s, the stench of uncollected rubbish, the dead unburied, honest men persuaded or coerced into fighting for unattainable goals. With the rate of inflation around 7 per cent, pay claims for 20, 30 and even 40 per cent increases proliferated. And, amid all this, the Ford Motor Company actually settled for 17 per cent and a left-wing rebellion in the Commons prevented sanctions being imposed on them. The firm impression given to the public was of a government wholly incapable of governing. In March 1979 the government lost a motion of confidence in the House of Commons and resigned. The Conservatives won the succeeding election by a substantial majority and Mrs Thatcher became Great Britain's fifty-first prime minister.

It is one of the ironies of politics that the old Labour Party was created by the trade unions towards the end of the nineteenth century and destroyed by the trade unions towards the end of the twentieth century. I wonder which middle class group will kill off New Labour? Could it be the Liberal Democrats or a revitalized Tory Party (perhaps in the guise of the 'English Motorists' Party')? And will we, like our American cousins, end up with only two national political parties distinguishable from each other only by their rhetoric and their symbols? We shall see.

But that is enough of this heavy stuff, first a tribute. As seen from below the stairs Jim Callaghan was a first-class politician (and a very nice man) who was overwhelmed by circumstances beyond even his control. Thinking back to those days, an episode that reveals a lot about his calibre was when someone approached him, in a panic, with a request for an immediate decision on subject X. The response was, 'If you want an instant answer it is "no". If you want a considered answer you must give me the facts and allow me enough time to consider them properly.'

And there is one more, which harks back to the one I told about John Eden some chapters back. The PM was visiting Liverpool at a time when the Militant Tendency was very active in that town and current left-wing propaganda focused on a march against unemployment. The atmosphere became tense with much loud heckling. Jim had foreseen this and had arranged for representatives of the local Ministry of Labour job centre to be present. Once they were in position the PM invited each heckler personally to 'give your name and address to one of those men over there with clipboards

THE RT. HON. BARONESS THATCHER, OM, PRIME MINISTER 1979–90

and they will see that you are put in touch with suitable job vacancies.' The mob melted away like the snow in spring.

And I have a poignant memory of Denis Healey. As we approached the Christmas recess in the middle of the 'winter of discontent' Denis, who chaired one of 'my' committees, asked me if we needed another meeting before the New Year?

'I would like to reserve a slot for one,' said I carefully avoiding the question.

'Why?' asked Denis (who incidentally was one of my two favourite prime ministers who never were, the other being Norman Tebbit).

'Because,' said I, 'our committee has met 99 times in the past 12 months, which, so far as I can check, is a peacetime record. One more before the end of the year and we're into the record books with a century!'

'Expletive deleted' does not do justice to Denis's reaction, but it was forceful.

I still think it was a good idea!

Meanwhile, before turning to the Thatcher years I must intrude one more bit of my personal history. The reader will remember that in 1976 I turned down a job as director general of the energy directorate general of the European Commission. In 1978 lightning struck twice and the same job came up for grabs again when the incumbent Welshman announced his forthcoming retirement. This time I let my willingness to take the job on be known and all seemed to be going my way. The president of the Commission was Roy Jenkins and I was led to believe, truthfully or not, that I had his backing. Unfortunately, Len Williams's retirement was postponed at the last moment and Roy Jenkins's term came to an end before decisions were taken. All bets were then off and the new president of the Commission (from Luxembourg) sanctioned the appointment of an English candidate from the Commission's own permanent staff. The reason given was that the Commission's own staff was restive at the continued 'parachuting' of national civil servants into the senior jobs in the Commission and that the new appointment was a token of good intent. Given the secrecy that surrounds these matters the truth is most unlikely to emerge and, in 99 cases out of 100, I am temperamentally inclined to prefer the cock-up to the conspiratorial theory of events. Nevertheless, in this case, with hindsight, I could believe an explanation that saw strengthening the grip of the permanent staff on the bureaucratic machine as a potent means of quelling internal dissent to the longer-term federalist ambitions of some member states and bureaucracies.

29

The World Turned Upside Down

In May 1979 Mrs Thatcher won the general election with a substantial majority and her first administration took office. The Cabinet Office, like all government departments, had as a matter of routine prepared briefs to guide all likely new governments on the immediate tasks they would face on taking office. These included analyses of the steps needed to flesh out and give life to their election programmes. This is a normal part of Whitehall's preparations for a change of administration and reflects its long experience that most new governments come to office knowing what their objectives are but that few have given real thought to how best to achieve them. Mrs Thatcher's accession to power was different. Her government had devoted a good deal of time and effort in opposition to preparing detailed plans and these were presented to officials as *faits accomplis* rather than as outline agendas. This situation presented no problems to the officials. To us, as in 1964, the advent of a government that knew its own mind was a relief, not a burden. Of course, as in 1964, there was an early problem of achieving trust between ministers and their officials. In 1964 the incoming Labour government thought that all (or at any rate most) senior civil servants were Tories at heart. And in 1979 the incoming Tory government thought that most officials were at best wet Liberals and at worst dyed in the wool socialists. The reality that most officials are apolitical pragmatists is very hard for politicians of any stripe to comprehend.

Nevertheless, mutual suspicion did not survive closer acquaintance. A famous dinner given by the PM to the assembled mandarins, while infuriating Mrs Thatcher, made quite clear (if clarity were needed) who was in charge; and, despite individual misgivings, most people pitched in to the new world with enthusiasm. Among the many facets of this revolution the areas that stand out in my mind are monetarism, privatization, trade union law, and efficiency in government — all against the backcloth of a return to the supremacy of the free market. It is not the purpose of this book to chronicle the development of public policy under the leadership of Queen Margaret. That must await the opening of the records and, almost certainly, another scribe. But a few general comments may shed a little light.

Monetarism

The theory here was that control of the behaviour of the economy of the country could be best achieved by controlling the supply of money available in the economy. If that were done, and the right signals given, the market could be left to take care of the detail without intervention by the state. In a sense, the monetarist doctrines echoed the old truisms of the so-called 'quantity theory of money' but carried the analysis forward from description to action. The difficulty came in determining how to turn theory into practice — in short, which levers to pull or which buttons to press — or, indeed, at a fundamental mechanical level, how to measure the amount of money in circulation so as to chart success or failure. In the event, the main levers/buttons turned out to be the familiar ones of the rate of interest, the level of taxation and the level of public spending. It is fascinating to note that the word 'monetarism', which was used almost as a swearword in the 1980s, has now disappeared from the political vocabulary.

Privatization

It was also clear that the process of economic renewal required a loosening of the structural barriers to change and adaptation — many of which were imposed by the state. Chief among these were the inbuilt inefficiencies of public ownership that bedevilled the proper working of wide areas of our national economy. It is an interesting thought that, when Mrs Thatcher came to power, 30 per cent of the working population of this country was employed in the public services or the nationalized industries. We were well down the road to a collectivized socialist state — and there were small but strong and well-organized forces on the left of the political spectrum who wanted to push us the rest of the way.

Those of my readers who treasure the inanities of some of the wealthier intellectual supporters of socialism* will recall that, in the 1930s the Webbs went to the Soviet Union and issued their famous (and fatuous) judgement that they had looked at the future 'and it works'. We, too, had now looked at a collectivist future in our own backyard and all the evidence showed that it did not work and, as became progressively more apparent, it did not work in the communist world either. The reality turned out to be that publicly owned enterprises, wherever situated, were too often seen by politicians as instruments of political, rather than economic, policy and by their staffs as existing for their benefit and not that of their customers. Any modern visitor

---

* The same people whose Bloomsbury ancestors translated the Internationale into such English as 'makes an end to the age of cant'. Can you imagine the revolutionary chitchat? *First revolutionary*: 'What's "cant" Fred?' *Second revolutionary*: 'You must be joking, Charley.'

to the communist or post-communist east will have had direct experience of this — as indeed will anyone who has experienced the tender mercies of, for example, the direct labour services of a loony left local council. In consequence 'privatization' became the order of the day (and, moreover, once its success was seen, spread like wildfire around the world). Indeed, it is among the manifold ironies of the death of socialism that many communist apparatchiks turned capitalist and grew rich on the back of the privatization that became possible once the old system was, as they no doubt put it, 'cast into the dustbin of history'.

It is worth noting that privatization took place at three levels. The first occurred internally to the undertaking or enterprise concerned. It had, of course, long been a commonplace of the thinking of private sector management to replace in-house services like cleaning, catering or the provision of security guards with external contracts for their supply by specialist firms. This process — 'contracting out' in the jargon — was easily and effectively transferred to the public sector despite strong opposition from some of the trade unions involved. However, the advantages of contracting out were so obvious that the wagon began to roll in a dramatic way. Central government, for example, embraced the, to them, new doctrines with the enthusiasm of converts when the scale of the potential benefits became apparent. The key discoveries for many were that the savings came, not only from the expected competition between suppliers for the work, but from the massive reduction in overhead costs that could be achieved once it was no longer necessary actively to manage the hived-off employees. No national insurance or pension contributions needed to be made; no supervision of staff was necessary; if staff were absent sick, finding stand-ins was the contractor's problem; and so on. If the contractor fulfilled his obligations he got paid. If he did not he was replaced by another contractor. The task of management was much eased.

The second element in privatization was to emulate the common private sector practice of reviewing fixed assets with a view to disposing of those, like under-performing subsidiaries, derelict land or empty buildings, that were not earning their keep. This practice was largely unknown in the public sector (British Rail under Dr Beeching was a notable exception). The reasons for this were many and varied. They ranged from simple inertia to the protection of private (and trade union) interests and the inbuilt reluctance of the Treasury to allow departments to keep, as an incentive, all or part of the proceeds of sales.

The third level of privatization came when whole industries and organizations were hived off. The techniques varied greatly from the sale of shares in the successor company to the sale of the business as a going concern. Whatever route was chosen the end result was a substantial flow of funds to the Exchequer or a reduction in the outflow of money as the government no longer needed to subsidize failure. Of course some ex-nationalized businesses were monopolies or quasi-monopolies. New mechanisms had to be devised to prevent such businesses from exploiting their customers. But, by and large, the resulting problems were successfully overcome. It is an interesting thought that what these new arrangements were doing, in effect, was resurrecting in a modern guise the regulatory arrangements of our Victorian ancestors when they set out to curb the natural monopolies of what were then known as the public utilities. There is, I suspect, material for another Ph.D. here.

Although the UK has taken privatization a long way there is still a lot of mileage to be got out of the public sector's remaining assets by any government with the courage to tackle the ideologues and the public sector unions head on. Luckily, the present Labour government has shown (perhaps not surprisingly for an avowedly middle-class party) that it has no ideological hang-ups about privatization. But will they have the courage to go the last mile by privatizing schools and hospitals? The last Tory government never quite got this far although NHS trusts, the 'internal market' and grant maintained schools went some way to introducing market disciplines into the Luddite practices and outlook of the mass trade unions of the medical, teaching and local government trade unions.

Of course, any attempt to change one iota of the practices, good, bad or indifferent, of the NHS runs head on into fundamentalist fervour. Certain 'principles' will be identified that were allegedly carved in stone by the founding fathers of the NHS. And among those identified as at risk will (I bet) be one that says that NHS treatment should be free at the point where it is delivered to the patient. Leaving aside the awkward facts that neither dental treatment nor drugs are 'free' it is, in fact, easy to envisage a system where the patient pays nothing and his or her fees are paid for them to a private hospital by some central agency. Not only is this done as a matter of daily routine by the medical insurance companies in the UK but the German equivalent of the NHS actually buys medical treatment for its clients abroad (including in the UK and no doubt in other countries) as a means of ironing out peaks and troughs in the demands for its services. As so often, self-interest masquerades as principle with the real trouble having less to do with the ideology of the NHS than with the interests of the apparatchiks of the mass unions of the NHS support staff. After all, the power, pay, perks and pensions they enjoy depend critically on the survival of mass unionism and a single monolithic employer. Fragmentation of either (as is happening to a degree with the advent of 'agencies' as the employer of some civil servants) would leave many of them as not very saleable flotsam on the labour market. Incidentally, it is an interesting thought that the NHS is the second largest employer in Europe outranked only by the Red Army. Both are, it would seem, too big for efficient management.

As for schools, the reluctance of the leaders of the new Labour Party to send their children to their local comprehensive schools demonstrates the failure of the old system. Couple this with the spectacular success of the grant maintained schools introduced by the last Conservative government — a success that rested on removing the dead hand of local government and local politics from the education system — and the case for fundamental reform is made. In saying this, I speak as the one-time governor of a local state school before, during and after its transition to GM status. In this (post-retirement) incarnation I learned many lessons not the least of which was that, while the apparatchiks of the teaching unions were motivated by pressure to protect their least capable members (15,000 pretty well useless according to the prime minister), their local authority equivalents rightly saw their own *raison d'être* as under direct threat.

Trade Unions

A good case can be made out that the British trade unions, whatever their early merits, have on balance damaged the interests of the working class particularly in the period since the First World War. A major contributory factor to this process has been the nature and rigidity of trade union laws and privileges inherited from the past. These started life as an attempt to protect the weak but degenerated into protective mechanisms for the misuse of monopoly power. As for trade union law, the reforms of the Thatcher years will almost certainly endure — after all, the leaders of the 'new' Labour Party know perfectly well why they were excluded from power for the 18 years from 1979 to 1997. And, of course, for all the talk of 'anti-trade union' laws, what really happened was that the flimflam got stripped away and the old fashioned law of contract resumed its place centre stage. There almost seems to be a conspiracy to keep quiet about this elemental fact. But what can be simpler or more defensible than the proposition that it takes two to make a bargain and if one party to an agreement breaks it, the other party is thereby relieved of any obligation to honour it? The fact that industrial relations agreements in the UK, unlike those in the USA, are not legally binding in themselves does not alter this situation. Those employees who break a contract of employment, written or implicit, by taking industrial action are in effect tendering their resignations and must not be surprised if their employer takes up their offer. Although the circumstances were not the same (US civil servants are forbidden by law to strike) the moment of truth came, I believe, when, in the USA, President Reagan sacked all the striking members of the federal air traffic control system and set about (successfully) finding replacements.

Efficiency in Government

Efficiency in government I will deal with in its due place later in this book when I recount a little of my own hands-on experience of seeking the Holy Grail. For the moment, however, let us stick with the secretariat.

Relations with Ministers

Central to the task of the secretariat was our relationship with the prime minister — and hers with her ministerial colleagues. Four episodes will give the flavour. First, her response to a ministerial colleague who was asked, at very short notice, to come to a small meeting she was calling to sort out some problem or other, and who demurred on the grounds of an unavoidable prior engagement — 'no problem; the fewer the people the easier it is to take decisions.' If Harry S. Truman had been looking down at that moment, he would have smiled.

Second, was her endearing habit of remembering, not what

had happened in the past, but what she had intended to happen. Not always quite the same thing but, unlike Labour ministers, the Tories rarely looked back at the records.

The prime minister could be, and was, abrasive with both her colleagues and her political enemies (insofar as the two could be distinguished) but her loyalty to her friends was intense and her reliance on the sheer professionalism of the secretariat led by John Hunt and Robert Armstrong in my day and by Robin Butler thereafter, was absolute. She had, of course, seen the secretariat in action when she had been a member of Ted Heath's government in the early 1970s and her good friend, confidant and deputy, Willie Whitelaw, had great experience of the ways of Whitehall and no doubt gave her good advice. Thus, it became clear very quickly that she was prepared to rely on us to do our job properly and to play the game by its longstanding rules. We got the odd complaint about the length of our minutes (we were all conscious of the need to serve both Whitehall and history) but it was about as serious as an injunction by the sergeant major of his air force or naval equivalents to 'get your hair cut' — a clear sign that if that was all she had to complain about we were doing quite well.

Finally, the first time my number two and I came into business contact with our new PM was in her very early days. The occasion was when a committee she chaired was due to take a paper on the annual settlement of the rate support grant to be given to local authorities in the coming year. This is a very complex subject and my colleague, who was a considerable expert on the problems, having handled them in the Treasury, wrote a very full brief on the issues to be resolved. The day after the brief had reached the PM he and I were summoned to her presence to discuss it. The PM opened up by telling us, with a quizzical look in her eye, that it was the first time in her career when the brief she was given on a subject exceeded in length the paper it was commenting upon. That said, there then followed a very thorough discussion that proved to us that she had read (and well understood) both the paper and our commentary upon it (which was not the secretariat's universal experience of all the ministers with whom we dealt).

One further point needs to be made before we leave this tricky area to future historians. Although Margaret Thatcher was our first lady prime minister we had, of course, had a number of lady ministers of all political shades over the years. And, in my experience they got treated as well or as badly as if they were honorary men (that useful fiction beloved of Muslim countries adapting to a new and difficult world). The difference with Mrs Thatcher was that she was not only female but also, without any question, the *boss*. In the eyes of her male colleagues, therefore, she not only qualified for the courtesies due from well brought-up males, but also to the deference due to one's commanding officer. Given that the cabinet contained a high proportion of ex-military types, the habits of a lifetime died hard. Of course, the situation was not always easy for either gender, but to get the flavour of the schizophrenic possibilities, try lifting your hat to, and swearing at, the same person at the same time.

And just to show that we still enjoyed ourselves, the day came in 1980 when Sir Kenneth Berrill, head of the Central Policy Review Staff and a noted ex-academic, shook the dust of Whitehall off his feet *en route* to the City. His staff (who like the rest of us greatly enjoyed Ken's company) paid him the compliment of preparing an elaborate parting joke. It had become known that, like all newcomers to his bit of the City, Ken would be required to pass a simple examination before taking up his new post. The joke was a spoof examination paper, which included two questions that have remained in my mind ever since. They are:

- 'The Prime Minister writes you a note about some problem on which you scribble "I wish she wouldn't get her knickers in a twist." Inadvertently, a copy of your comment finds its way to her and she asks for an explanation. Produce a draft reply in not more than a hundred words'; and

- 'From the soup provided, create life.'

Another episode, hilarious in retrospect, which occurred to me came when I was invited to speak to the Staff College at Camberley about the machinery of government. I prepared a suitable text and took it to the college in my briefcase along with other items that would enable me to do some work in the car. On arrival I got my text from my bag, which I then deposited in the cloakroom for safekeeping. And so off I went to the auditorium where I started my spiel. Ten minutes later when I was just getting into my stride, a sergeant sidled up to me on stage and said, 'Excuse me interrupting, Sir, but your bag is ticking.' As soon as I decently could I excused myself and went with the sergeant to the field where my bag now rested under a tree. I was mightily puzzled and the army was awaiting a bomb squad that would blow it up unless I could remember a plausible explanation for the weird noise issuing from its bowels. Luckily, the penny then dropped and, feigning a nonchalance I did not feel, I got out my key and opened the offending bag. Fortunately for me, I had guessed right. It was my habit to carry around with me a small hand-held dictating machine, which had somehow got knocked on by the movement of my bag. The machine had then come to the end of its tape where it proceeded to go 'tick, tick, tick' to let me know that a fresh tape was needed. The army was desperately polite about the whole thing, though I suspect it confirmed its worst fears about ex-naval civil servants. A double whammy no less!

The only other public event in the early history of Mrs Thatcher's administration to which I need to draw attention as background to my narrative, is the civil service strike that lasted from March to July 1981. The origins of the strike lay in the government's unilateral decision to suspend, for the 1981 pay round, the system of pay determination that had been in use for the civil service for the preceding 25 years following the report of the 'Priestley' Royal Commission of 1953. This system was built around the concept of 'fair comparisons' with outside pay levels and had, by 1980, seen elaborate mechanisms put in place for quantifying the basic data and drawing conclusions from it. However, the new government had philosophical doubts about the validity of this system as well as facing the need for tight restraints on public expenditure. In the event, the government suspended the pay research procedures for the 1981 settlement and refused arbitration on the total amount of the settlement. The civil service unions accordingly embarked on a campaign of selective industrial action, which began on 9 March 1981 and continued until 31 July 1981.

Again it is not for me to embark on a detailed analysis of the strike — that can only properly be done when the books are open to public scrutiny — but suffice it to say that the civil service unions played a very skilful hand, wholly within the law, which enabled most of their members to remain on the public payroll. At the same time the government had the great advantage, which all governments enjoy, of financing the costs of the strike entirely at the expense of the taxpayer. (As an aside, it is remarkable how many people forget the elementary fact that governments have no money. Every penny they spend comes from other people and most of it is extracted from them by force. Think about it every time you read 'government spends more on X' — it does not, you do whether you want to or not.)

As it happens, I left the secretariat before the strike was over. However, before leaving the subject of our relations with the PM, I should cast ahead in time a little to refer to a private event that throws a perhaps unexpected light on the character of Mrs Thatcher and deserves recording on that account. It happened that one of the messengers who work at No 10 was due to retire and he asked the PM's principal private secretary (by then Robin Butler) for permission to invite a few friends into the building for a retirement party. Robin mentioned the retirement to Mrs Thatcher who promptly adopted the event as her own. The venue of the party now became the staterooms at No 10 (one of its hidden treasures) and the resources of the office were put behind it. When the day came the prime minister spent over an hour talking to the guests and generally making sure that all went with a swing. The point, however, is that this very kindly gesture to an old and faithful employee was made entirely without publicity of any kind.

It is very easy to follow leaders like that.

30

À La Lanterne

In April 1981, in the middle of the civil service strike, my term at the secretariat expired and I was posted to the Civil Service Department. The understanding was that, if all went well, I stood a very good chance of succeeding John Herbecq as second permanent secretary in that department and as such would be its second in command. The permanent secretary of the department was Ian Bancroft, who also served as head of the Home Civil Service. Meanwhile, I would learn my trade (I had a lot of experience of strikes but precious little of run of the mill personnel work) while standing back from the detail of the current civil service pay dispute, which would broadly be left to those already immersed in it.

However, it soon became apparent that I would be responsible for putting Humpty Dumpty back together again when the strike was finally over. Indeed, someone once told me that I had gained a bit of a reputation as Whitehall's 'fireman' although at the time it felt more like being the little Dutch boy whose finger was stuffed (implausibly) in the hole in the dyke and who must have got very wet. As part of this process I soon found myself deeply involved in the detail of the setting up, and later of the servicing, of the Megaw Inquiry into 'the principles and the system by which the remuneration of the non-industrial civil service should be determined'. Sir John Megaw was a distinguished judge and the setting up of his inquiry a month before the strike ended was a major step towards bringing it to a close. The other main element in the settlement was a government promise to allow arbitration on the pay settlement for 1982.

The process of my education kept me usefully employed over the following months. Included in my activities during this period was an educational exploration I undertook into the pay structures of other civil services and major employers of clerical labour at home and overseas. I undertook this work, which in a sense represented unfinished business from the Fulton Report of 1968, as personal preparation for the battles on pay systems that were already raging about my ears. I undertook it also because of my firm belief that the besetting sin of the British way of politics and administration was its tendency to reinvent the wheel. As I have already explained this stemmed in part from our bad habit of moving staff (and ministers) around frequently and so losing the benefits of continuity of experience; and in part from the lack of resources we (to be precise ministers and Treasury) were prepared to commit to recording the lessons to be learned from our own history let alone that of others. But it is very relevant that a competent management consultant will begin a piece of research into a new subject with a trawl of the literature so as to discover what useful experience is on record. It is also relevant that the same problems of administration crop up in most societies: what differ are the solutions adopted by each in the light of their own circumstances and traditions. Lifting up one's eyes to the hills brings more than religious understanding.

I think the fact that impressed me most was that, no doubt because of the minutiae of the pay research process, the British civil service paid its staffs by reference to many hundreds of different pay scales (1400 at the time of the Fulton Report) with thousands of separate pay points. By contrast, for example, the US federal civil service at that time grouped more than one and a quarter million 'general service' staff within 18 different pay scales with only 165 separate pay points. Other comparisons in the public and private sectors showed similar contrasts. This fragmentation of the British service imposed substantial administrative penalties, for example in the cross posting of staff of different disciplines. It also posed a major barrier to progress, as recommended by Fulton and accepted by government, in moving towards a unified (and much simplified) grading structure for the bulk of the service. It was the practice in those days for the mandarins to gather each summer for a few days' private discussion of problems of common concern and a senior colleague interested in grading issues and I were invited to tell the meeting about our latest thinking in this area. The resulting discussion was lively and generated a good deal of interest. It was clear that the climate was now ripe for further progress to be achieved.

The French Civil Service Pay System

At the time of the Fulton Report, the received wisdom among practitioners was to regard the French as the leaders of administrative fashion particularly where training was concerned and I, too, shared that view. Little interest was, however, expressed in their pay, grading and personnel management systems generally and hard information on these was difficult to come by. I, for example, was unable to lay my hands on a comprehensive account of the French pay system although the pay system of the EEC, modelled upon it, gave cause for alarm. The lack of information was, however, remedied a year or so later by research carried out for the Megaw Inquiry and reproduced in volume two of its report. This described a system of an order of magnitude more complex than ours and, I suspect, inspired more by Machiavelli than muddle. Two quotations from the Megaw Report will give the flavour.

A former director of the École Nationale d'Administration (ENA) is recorded as commenting that:

The French civil service is unhappily characterized by its compartmentalization, which is reaching manifestly silly proportions; the existence of 800 [technical] corps, of 3000 grades, of exclusive rights to numerous categories of jobs for members of particular corps are among the principal signs of this. The personnel function is devoting much of its time and effort to managing this unnecessarily complex and rigid structure. As for the civil servants themselves, surrounded by these strict rules, they are not always inclined towards effort or initiative, since their careers are largely predetermined by their allegiance to a corps.

And later, on pay, the study explains:

To base pay, derived from the individual's current position on the grille [a pay matrix linking all grades and specialities], is added various allowances and premiums. These complicate matters considerably, since there are literally thousands of different allowances permitted by statute and full details of them are not readily available. Some are not discretionary and are enjoyed by nearly all civil servants. Others are either entirely within the discretion of management or depend on specified criteria of eligibility. Some are taxable or pensionable, others not. Indeed, some are taxable and pensionable if paid by one department, but not by another. Allowances and premiums account for as much as 50 per cent of base salary though 10 per cent is more typical. Two allowances are almost universally applicable, the Local Allowance and the Family Allowance. The Local Allowance is paid as a percentage of basic pay according to a tariff of 4, 5 or 7 per cent. The Family Allowance is paid in addition to the state family allowance available under Social Security provisions. It consists partly of a fixed amount per child and partly of a salary related element. As to the rest of the allowance system there are premiums for educational qualifications, special skills, unsocial hours, overtime, productivity or efficiency, individual special merit, certain types of work, and many other situations and contingencies. No central record is kept of the payment of premiums, as they are the responsibility and prerogative of individual Ministries.

Add to this little lot the fact that the pay received by senior French civil servants is a state secret and you have (as in Brussels — but minus the secrecy) a system designed by the workers for the workers (bearing in mind, of course, that, especially in France, some workers are more equal than others).

Abolition of the Civil Service Department

And then, in the autumn of that year, the tumbrels rolled. Shock! Horror! The Prime Minister had used her powers to abolish the Civil Service Department (CSD) and redistribute its duties to the Treasury and a new creation — the Cabinet Office (management and personnel office).* The Establish-

---

* The powers of the prime minister derive from custom not law. Indeed, the *Statute Book* barely mentions the office of PM at all. A hunt through the records in the 1980s only unearthed a reference to the prime minister in a statute authorizing ministerial pensions. But, of course, the PM is a virtual dictator so far as the government is concerned. Despite the legal black hole, he or she alone has the right to hire and fire ministers; he or she alone has the right to carve up and rearrange the machinery of government; and he or she alone has total command of the honours and public appointments machine. Add to that the fact that modern prime ministers are also leaders of their parties and Robert Walpole (our first prime minister, holder of the eighteenth century office of patronage secretary and author of the dictum that 'every man has his price') would be proud of them.

ment was shaken as one more pillar of the corporate state came crashing to the ground. As for me, being but newly arrived in the arcane world of personnel management, I watched silently as the drama unfolded and an irresistible force met a very moveable object. Moreover, being blessed with a mind that thrives on vivid (and often disrespectful) illustration, I hunted around for a quotation, or a song, that might suitably reflect the stunned reaction of the bureaucratic and trade union establishments. I found one in an old Victorian music hall ditty that tells the sad story of a young mother bathing her baby who turns to pick up the soap. And then:

> She only turned wound for a minnit
> But Oh when she turned back!
> The baby 'ad utterly wanished, wanished completely away!
> She cwyed 'Oh where is my baby?'
> She erred an Angel say
> 'Your baby 'as gorn dahn the plug 'ole!'

The whole ending with a rousing rendition of

> Not lorst but gorn before!

Exhausted by that difficult spelling I will make haste to move on. But before doing so I must make the point that the work of the CSD did not evaporate with the department but had to be continued in some other corner of the Whitehall woods. Broadly speaking, the Treasury took pay and pensions and the Cabinet Office took the 'people' issues like recruitment, training, grading and so on. The division and destination of the work made good sense both politically and administratively. On the political side no one could accuse the Treasury of being soft on pay — hair shirts are, or were, standard Treasury issue. The division also made sense administratively because neither organization would have been physically capable, at ministerial level at any rate, of handling the full load of the CSD's work in addition to its old duties. In fact, the major changes in the machinery of government made relatively little difference to the staff. Letterheads had to be reprinted, chains of command shifted, rooms moved. But all this was par for the course and a natural outcome once it is recognized that the work has to be done somewhere and preferably by staff who know what they are about. Nevertheless, there were changes and it was these that tempted me to think, not only of Victorian music hall ditties, but also of that great song of the French Revolution — *Ça Ira* — and the glorious rendition of it by Edith Piaff. When she sang *Les Aristos à la Lanterne* she clearly meant it and so, figuratively, did Maggie.

Finally, there is my funny/courageous story, which comes from the last months of the CSD. This involved our then minister (Christopher Soames) and an undersecretary called Geoffrey. The minister noticed that the final pay settlement after the strike gave the troops a smidgeon more in percentage terms than the senior staff had been given at the outset of the strike. Would they, he ruminated, want more to catch up with the rest of the service? A hundred years of experience and training went into the reply. 'No Minister,' said Geoff, 'I think they would prefer to retain their justified sense of grievance.'

In the reshuffle I was sent to the Treasury and was given responsibility for pay and pensions.

31

The Labourer is Worthy of His Hire

When I arrived in the Treasury I found myself in an alien culture. In all the departments I had served in, the making of policy was very much a matter that engaged the responsibility of different groups of individuals. Ideas would come in from outside or through ministers and MPs or upwards from the division concerned. If other divisions, like finance, had a legitimate interest they would be brought into discussion but essentially the preparation of proposals and priorities lay between the responsible division, senior line management above it and the appropriate ministers. The Treasury was different. The approach to policy making was collegiate. Once a week the senior staff gathered and discussed current problems or proposals for new or modified policy stances. Of course, at the end of the day, the most senior staff shouldered responsibility for the advice tendered to ministers. But the whole aim of the preparatory process was to seek a consensus view. With the very sharp reduction in the number of senior Treasury staff in recent years it could be that the old ways have changed. In any event, the whole area of decision taking in Whitehall can, I think, be offered up as yet another potentially fruitful subject for academic study.

It is not my intention in this work to probe deeply into

policy issues or to defend or criticize particular decisions. That will only be possible when the books are open. All I aim to do is to give my readers some feel of what it was like to be an official close to the heart of government through a very turbulent stretch of our nation's history. As it happens, my two years in the CSD and Treasury from the spring of 1981 to the spring of 1983 were exceptionally eventful. Four issues dominated – the Megaw Inquiry; the arbitration process of 1982; the negotiated pay settlement of 1983; and the pressure to modify the civil service pension scheme.

The Megaw Inquiry

The Megaw Inquiry faced the difficult task of reconciling the irreconcilable. On the one hand stood the government's employees who placed great faith in the 'fair'* pay system introduced in the 1950s on the recommendation of a prestigious Royal Commission (the Priestley Commission) and endorsed by the equally prestigious Fulton Committee in

---

* The concept of 'fairness' was a source of much emotion during the civil service strike and subsequently. This was partly a generation thing with both the wartime and prewar generations imbued with the concept from an early age. Its origins no doubt rested on the importance given to 'fair play' in the games that were the national obsession of children and adults alike in the days before television. But the siege mentality of the war years added great weight to 'fair shares'. Thus, conscription was 'fair' because it tended to equalize the chances of being killed by the enemy; and rationing was 'fair' because all suffered equally; and the new 'Beveridge' social security and health systems were 'fair' because they narrowed the impact of inequalities of income distribution on social conditions. Of course, there was an element of 'New Jerusalem' hype in all this but the massive vote for Labour in the general election of 1945 reflected a genuine national mood and set of value judgements. But by the 1980s the mood was changing or had changed. In 1982 I attended a graduation ceremony addressed by the well-known Canadian businessman Sir Graham Day. Among other wise words, he warned the assembled students 'Be under no illusion. It ain't fair out there.'

1968. Moreover, complexity apart, the British system was founded on the same principle of comparability with the private sector used by that pillar of free market capitalism — the United States of America — though in the American case the comparisons were not binding. The staff felt that the assault on their 'rights' was inspired more by anti-civil service sentiment than by economic theory and that the civil service had been selected for assault as a populist bogey. The government, on the other hand, strongly denied political motives and maintained firmly that the greatest good of the greatest number could only be achieved by giving full rein to market forces in the settlement of pay as in all other economic activities.

Incidentally, in the private margins of this dispute I enjoyed pulling the legs of the senior people of the Federation of British Industry by telling them that one of the strengths of the comparability system was that it put civil service pay firmly in the hands of British industry and commerce. If they were responsible in their pay settlements the civil service would have no choice but to follow suit automatically. The responses I got would have led Corporal Jones to say 'They don't like it, up 'em, Sir!'

In its findings the Megaw Inquiry noted that the objective of a pay system was to 'recruit, retain and motivate' a staff of adequate calibre 'to perform efficiently the duties required of them'. To this end they recommended a system of 'informed collective bargaining' within limits set by comparability data (rather than one in which the outcome was determined by such data). They also, *inter alia*, recommended the introduction of a system of performance related pay and of actual contributions to pensions (rather than the notional offsets to pay then in use). They also shot a popular fox by concluding that 'it is not possible to put a precise figure on the value of civil service job security or to make a specific deduction on account of job security, but job security should be taken into account as an unquantifiable factor in negotiations.' Altogether, it was a judicious report that became less and less relevant as the civil service was fragmented over the next decade.

The Arbitration of 1982

The pay settlement date of 1982 came round and with it the need to face the promised arbitration procedure. I led the government team and was expected to do most of the talking. Two strong memories stand out: the sheer volume of preparation needed and the argument about the purpose of pay.

Preparation was pure hard graft. As leader I would be expected to react off the cuff to points made in the course of the hearing. This meant both anticipating questions that might be posed and having a firm grasp of the relevant facts. Of course my troops and I went over the ground together, several times, and teased out a great deal of the material we thought we would need. Thus far, it was just an exercise in intelligent prediction and anticipation. The difficult bit, however, was to get all this stuff organized so that it could be found in a hurry, and then getting as much as possible of it into my head. I remember the last weekend before the 'off' lying on the floor of the conservatory at home (for some reason I do — or did — all of my best work lying down with a cushion under my elbow), smoking like a chimney and trying to keep my cool. In the end, it worked at the cost of an enormous expenditure of nervous energy. I was particularly pleased, when it was all over, to be told by David Calcutt (the chairman of the Civil Service Arbitration Tribunal and a very distinguished member of the Bar), 'Peter, we'll make an advocate of you yet.' I mumbled some suitable reply but kept to myself the real response of, 'No way! Once is enough.'

The other sharp memory is of meeting the argument that the pay of the lowest grades of civil servant was, and on our proposals would remain, below the subsistence level recognized by the social security system. The reply was, of course, that we paid our people for the work they did irrespective of their economic or social circumstances. These latter factors were, I said, the province of children's allowances, family support and the other elements of social security system. To muddle them up with pay, I said, would be to distort the purpose of both. Pay was for work done. Social security payments were to meet social needs.

The unions jumped on these statements to claim that a heartless government's response to their just demands was that civil servants who felt underpaid should go on social security. This story followed me around for some time and gave me a strong fellow feeling for politicians who get tagged with similar distortions.

The Negotiation of 1983

The pay negotiation of 1983 was a fascinating experience. Not only was it my first major negotiation with the civil service unions but it took place against a background of confidence in me by my bosses — earned no doubt by the shared experience of Megaw and the arbitration of the preceding year. In short, although I was given a tough overall target at which to aim, and provided, of course, that I kept my ministerial and official superiors informed of what I was up to and sought their blessing where necessary, I was given a pretty free hand to develop my own strategy and to sort out the detail with the personnel experts of the relevant departments.

In the event, the strategy was a simple one. We constructed a pay offer based on a tactic used by Denis Healey years before for coping with difficult budgets. The sterner his message and the more meagre his resources, the more Denis splashed out with small concessions. That way, at least there were cheers mixed with the boos. Our version of this covered a lot of territory but examples were the creation of an intermediate zone for London weighting — thus reducing the height of the cliff drop in pay as the London weighting boundary was passed. Boundaries are always a nuisance, but one that made several hundred pounds difference in the salaries of staff doing identical jobs in offices situated on either side of the same road, cried out for change. Another was the provision of facilities for staff to get cheaper private medical insurance (without subsidy but making use of our weight in the market). And another was a recasting of the pay scales applicable to the clerical staff employed in local social security offices where the physical danger of the job led to very high and expensive levels of staff turnover.

The point, however, was not simply that each of our offers furthered a clear managerial objective but that they were volunteered without being asked for by the unions. This not only seized the initiative from their negotiators (which was the intention) but also, as one of the union team put it to me privately, caused them real problems (which to be honest I had not foreseen). As he put it to me, the 10 per cent of the members given a special offer put it quietly in their pockets and the 90 per cent left out complained bitterly about their leaders' neglect of their interests.

The other innovation we introduced was that, simultaneously with being given to the union leaders, our offer was put directly to the troops at a series of coordinated meetings across Whitehall. This compared with past practice when the offer was given to the union negotiators who passed it on to their rank and file with whatever spin they chose. This time we got our spin in first.

The negotiations then continued over several days with minor concessions being made on both sides. Then came the crunch. I said to them privately that I had used up all the leeway allowed me by the prime minister. From this point on '*ç'est la guerre*, Pussycat!' They asked my troops whether I had any leeway left and were told that, as they knew quite well, Maggie was a stubborn old so-and-so and the answer to their question was 'no'. We then, very secretly, dotted the i's and crossed the t's of an agreement. That done we moved to the final charade where they made speeches to their gallery and I made one to mine. They said, in effect, that the government made Alderman Gradgrind look like Mother Teresa, and I said that, on the contrary, our generosity made Father Christmas look like Scrooge. Nevertheless, despite the insults we both were able to say that the deal we had come to was the best available in the circumstances and (implicitly) that it was much better than a return to the barricades. So, with the job done, now let us get on with the work.

Index-Linked Pensions

One issue that remained alive during my overlapping jobs under the Conservatives in the secretariat, the CSD and the Treasury was the rumbling row about the enjoyment by the civil service of index-linked pensions. The origins were simple. The Middle Classes and particularly the small businessmen and women, shopkeepers and the self-employed generally, found that high inflation was very damaging to the income from annuities or government stock, which many of them relied on to support them in retirement. Of course, inflation sometimes worked to their advantage as house prices rose and the real value of any loans they had taken out fell sharply, but rational calculation is not a feature of bewildered or frightened people. What they saw was that the real value of the pensions of bureaucrats was protected and that 'their' government was doing nothing about it. More-over, the affected citizens provided a disproportionate share of the foot soldiers of the local Conservative parties, so that their cries for help could not be ignored by politicians whose future depended on them.

In the event, the government came up with a partial solution in the shape of index-linked bonds and also managed painfully to tackle the inflationary genie that lay at the root of the problem. But the real killer for the anti-bureaucrat brigade came from the dawning realization among politicians of all parties that the index-linked pension was not an unfair perk of bowler-hatted wimps but the cherished birthright of ministers of the Crown, members of parliament, all the gallant lads and lasses of the army, navy and air force, all the nurses and doctors employed by the National Health Service, all policemen, all local government employees, all teachers employed by the state and most of the employees of the nationalized industries. As I recall it, the total headcount came to more than seven million people, including a high proportion of the most articulate, argumentative and vocal members of our society. Add to that the often-overlooked fact that every citizen either received, or was in line to receive, an index–linked state pension and the abolition of index linking was a political suicide note waiting to be written.

Before leaving this fascinating subject let us take one more peek across the Channel where our French friends share with us the problem of protecting public sector incomes from inflation. The problem may be the same but their response to it differs markedly from ours. In the case of civil service pensions the French do not have index linking — nothing so crude. What they do is to link pensions to the pay of the man or woman who takes over your job when you retire. Your pension goes up each year by the same percentage as your successor's salary. Of course, this means that, in most years, your pension will increase by more than the rate of inflation so that you will share in the growing wealth of your society. It is an easy wicket to defend if you inherit the system, but expensive if you try to move to it given the inevitable knock on effect on the state pension (where we abandoned this humane alternative several crises back).

The French approach to retirement pensions generally also differs markedly from ours in institutional ways. Our non-state pension provision is largely a matter for the individual to arrange or for his or her employer to provide. This is not so in France where the company pension is largely unknown. Instead, under the supervision of the state, a number of very large specialist companies (*caisses*) have been set up to provide pensions for whole sectors of the economy. As a result, small shopkeepers say, all pay in to a common pension fund backed by the state that tops up its funds from time to time as circumstances require. The resulting pensions are index linked. So, there is no jealousy of the pampered officials but periodic financial problems as the politicians have to put the taxpayers money where their mouths are. Oh well! You can't have everything.

And so we proceed to the Cabinet Office (MPO).

32

Who Does What

In the spring of 1983 John Cassels, the second permanent
secretary who ran the Cabinet Office (Management and
Personnel Office), departed to take up the post of
director general of the National Economic Development
Office (known as NEDDY to its friends). I, in my turn, was
sent, on promotion, to the MPO to take John's place.

The Financial Management Initiative

When I got there the office was a hive of activity. In the
previous year the government had launched a financial management initiative designed to improve the allocation,
management and control of resources throughout central
government. With total public expenditure exceeding 43 per
cent of the gross domestic product, it was, the government
averred, essential that resources be used efficiently and
money spent wisely. The machinery for giving effect to this
mission was under construction and an explanatory white
paper was to be published later in the year. Meanwhile, the
training of staff in the new control and information systems
was in hand with the MPO masterminding the process of
'training the trainers'. Again this is not the forum for describing the new arrangements and systems in detail. Suffice
it to say that the heart of the operation was to achieve
clarity about who did what; what were the objectives of
their activities; who was accountable for the results achieved;

and what costs were incurred in achieving them. In addition, clarity was sought about who was responsible for the money spent; what freedom they had to take expenditure decisions without reference to higher authority; and what freedom they had to vary the pattern of their expenditure within the agreed total. If the new system had to be described in one sentence, it would be increased delegation of responsibility down the chains of command, an increased flow of meaningful information to senior management and more hands-on management at every level, up to and including ministers.

A few illustrations may give the flavour of what we were about. Thus one of my divisions was responsible for managing a common recruitment organization for much of Whitehall. Under the new dispensation it was quite clear that departments were free to use our organization for recruitment (on payment) or to recruit their own staffs directly from the market if they so wished. The same thing applied to training. The Civil Service College sold its services to departments, but its clients were also free to go round the corner to the local poly if they chose. While bringing a wide degree of freedom into the system, these changes made forecasting the financial results of the recruitment and training organizations very tricky, especially in the early days. The heads of these two organizations had small reserves at their disposal and freedom to modify their organizations to save money if they chose — provided always that they delivered the goods — and were only expected to come to me for help when they had exhausted all the other possibilities. In short, an appeal up the line for assistance, which used to attract a reply on the lines of 'what can I do to help?' now received a brutal 'so you've got a problem. What are you doing to solve it?' Of course, help was available thereafter, but only when senior management was satisfied that local management had really tried to cope.

At a different level, much time and effort were saved by delegating responsibility down the line. To take a simple example, if a window in a local office was broken pre-reform, the local manager would simply ring up the next layer of command and report the fault and then just sit back and await a visit from the area glazier or whatever. Post-reform he would have a fund for minor maintenance work and would simply ring up a local glazier and get the work done, pay for it from his fund and file the papers for the annual audit. Inevitably, such systems opened a door for minor fraud, but the vast majority of our employees were honest and the savings in bureaucracy, time, staff morale, hassle and cash more than outweighed any conceivable cost.

The search for a proper allocation of costs to users threw up some spectacular results. Thus, until reform it was common practice in Whitehall to regard the costs of public utilities like gas, water and electricity as, in effect, free goods. Meters were read and supplies paid for by the ministry that had physical possession of the meter, irrespective of changes in the allocation of buildings between departments or of the identity of the real end user. After all, it was all one pot wasn't it? Two examples from the MPO will show what I mean. When the CSD was formed it took over the old Admiralty building (which runs from Whitehall along the west side of Horse Guards Parade to The Mall and St James's Park). The one exemption from transfer was the wartime Citadel (the massive concrete bunker covered in ivy which abuts onto the Parade) because, at that time, this housed some Admiralty communications equipment. When in 1982 the Cabinet Office (MPO) took over a large part of the CSD it moved in its turn into the old Admiralty building little knowing (or to be frank caring) that the electricity consumption of the Citadel was being charged for on its meter. When this became apparent in the early days of my tenure I got the system rewired smartly so that the MoD could pay for its own teakettles or whatever.

The other example came from a building used by the Civil Service College just around the back from Victoria station.

As part of our new policy of monitoring and controlling expenditure we had a water meter installed in the building instead of paying on the old rating system. The results were staggering. Water consumption was sky high and way above anything we could identify. Investigation showed a massive water leak that had probably gone unnoticed for years. Now that the water board and we knew of it, repairs were quickly made to our mutual benefit.

Grading

The Fulton Committee had identified our complex grading structures for staff as a source of administrative weakness and cost. There were two sides to this. First, the pay structure we had inherited from the comparisons machine was a complex and expensive mess that cried out for reform. We were not in the same pickle as the French but we were too close for comfort. And second, the proliferation of grades raised major barriers in the way of cross-posting staff from discipline to discipline as Fulton had urged and to which the government was committed.

The pay problem was easily settled in principle (though not always in practice). One solution lay before us in the pay systems (believe it or not) of local authorities and teachers. Both operated pay structures built around a pay spine with a hundred or so pay points separated by a standard deviation (percentage or absolute) that could be assembled at will into pay scales of varying complexity. With this arrangement movement from one scale to another was simple and direct with no need for complicated rules of assimilation. The pay settlement of 1983 made a tentative beginning with the mammoth task of bringing order into chaos but showed clearly that real progress would require hard cash because no one could be required by law to accept a fall in pay so that, if all assimilation was to be upward, the cost could be high. Treasury reluctance to pay a steep price for an essentially unquantifiable gain was not unexpected. Nevertheless, as our politicians sometimes explained to us, apparent progress is often as useful as real movement. So, whatever the reality, we accompanied our moves on uniform grading with the introduction of grade numbers to identify rank instead of the '57 varieties' of secretary, which had gone before. As it happened, the diplomatic service had done the same thing many years before (they after all had only a limited number of specialities with which to cope). The only snag from the point of tidy-minded home service administrators was that the diplomats had one rank fewer than us so that grade for grade they looked more important than they were.

The other quirky result was that, as we had chosen grade one for the permanent secretaries, grade one A for the second permanent secretaries and grades two, three, four and so forth thereafter, Robert Armstrong and his FCO counterpart, who were superior to all other permanent secretaries, came out logically as grade zero. (I said 'zero' not 'Zorro' — though come to think of it?)

The problem of free movement between grades and specialities reflected, at least in part, the technical requirements of the tasks to be performed. We already had free movement in the most senior ranks (the so-called 'open structure') where the reality of the work was that administrative competence and leadership skills were the attributes most in demand. All jobs at the top had accordingly been opened up to all claimants with the necessary attributes. The problem lower down can be described crudely as being that, while it can be wasteful, but not impossible, to use a brain surgeon to do plumbing work, it would be abject folly to try and use a plumber as a brain surgeon. The problem really resolved itself into the age-old one of how to cope with boundaries? We got as far as getting uniform grading down to principal level (grade seven in the new jargon) but thereafter the issue was temporarily put on ice and only revived when I had left the service.

The Dead Hand of Parliament

I ought to begin this part of my work with an explanation. Had I been alive in the 1640s I would have fought for Parliament in the Civil War. Had I been alive in the 1770s I would have fought for the Yanks in the War of Independence. And had I been alive in Napoleon's time I would have fought for the English against tyranny. That said, let us return to the work in hand.

In the past the civil service has often been chided with having an old fashioned approach to management. Maybe so and perhaps things have got better since I left. But even in my day the fault was not entirely ours. Take, for example, the lunatic form of public finance imposed on us by Parliament, which insisted on doling out cash to ministries largely on an annual basis and which, moreover, made no distinction between current and capital spending. The resulting nonsenses were manifold. Departments developed squirrel complexes in which they hoarded potentially reusable assets so that, if they ever needed them again, they would not need to pay for them. An example arose in 1940 when the Home Guard was partially fitted out with ex-Boer War leather equipment, which had been lying in store for the best part of forty years. The hoarders would, of course, say that such examples justify their actions. But a great deal of useless junk was tucked away, expensively, alongside the potentially useful — including, I recall, stocks of computer printout paper that would only fit obsolete machines. Another consequence of Parliament's indifference or incompetence (I could never quite make up my mind which word applied) was that it generated a last minute scramble by those in charge of ministry funds to spend unused balances before the end of the financial year when the Treasury would do its best to claw them back. It is alleged, for example, that the old Ministry of Health piled up its warehouses with invalid chairs because these items were among the most readily available bits of medical kit that could be bought off the shelf in March.

Another example of costly distortions imposed by Parliament occurred in my old department, energy. Our main London headquarters on the banks of the River Thames was rented by government in the middle of the war. Forty years later it was still being rented although it could have been bought at any time in the intervening years had the cash been made available — and given the rise in rents and property values in those years the taxpayer would have made a tidy profit. Things have (I hope) got a bit better since my day, but a Ph.D. student could still usefully try and estimate the loss suffered by the taxpayer as a result of the unwillingness of Parliament to adopt the accounting and other business methods of the twentieth century. In the course of his or her studies, the Ph.D. student might also care to contemplate the odd fact that, while all other government expenditure is cash limited that of Parliament is not subject to this constraint. Could the motto of Parliament once more be 'Don't do as I do. Do as I tell you'?

Two other points of this kind need to be made and I will then shut up about it. The first relates to ministerial control of their departments. One thread leading to the FMI reforms described above was the initiative taken by Michael Heseltine on his appointment as secretary of state for the environment in the first Thatcher government. His business experience led him to propose and operate a ministerial information system (MINIS in the jargon of the day) that would enable him to keep a close eye on what was going on in his ministry and to exert pressure for change where he thought this necessary. The reforms of the early Thatcher years benefited from this experience but also showed up one inherent weakness in the British system. To work properly MINIS and similar arrangements required a substantial input from the departmental ministers concerned. Some, like Michael Heseltine, threw themselves wholeheartedly into the management game. Others did not. Some of these were even heard to mutter that they had not entered politics to run a chip shop; others found the task boring; and yet others were incapable of undertaking this kind of task. Given the way in which MPs and ministers are selected this is hardly surprising (the constituency selection committee meeting in a smoke filled room is most decidedly not looking for clones of Richard Branson to represent them). Indeed, we are actually very lucky that our system throws up enough talent to enable our successive governments to cope with the world in which we live as well as with the expectations of their supporters. But the more we proliferate the number of ministers (at June 1999 we had 113 of them drawn from both Houses, plus 23 parliamentary whips also drawn from both Houses) the more we will be drawing, very expensively, on the ranks of the unemployable. Perhaps the mistake is to pay ministers more than their parliamentary salaries. Or perhaps we should follow the American example and hire ministers from the market place instead of drawing them from the limited ranks of those politicians who manage to claw their way into Parliament.

The final point I would make is a warning against the quick fix gimmicks so beloved of academics and saloon bar pundits. A good example of what I mean is the attempt made by President Carter in the USA to adopt a popular academic nostrum of his day known as 'zero base budgeting' This was a proposal under which policy makers would not simply look at suggestions for additional expenditure at the margin — should we buy another battleship? — but should begin by asking 'do we need battleships at all? And if so how many?' This was a lovely idea. The only trouble with it was that looking at everything from the beginning took an enormous amount of time and staff effort and proved quite unmanageable within the time available. In reality, zero based budgeting never got much beyond zero plus a little bit. Of course the Americans, being American, dropped the idea stone dead as soon as it became clear it would not work.

Opening the Door

When I joined the MPO I had three years to go to retirement. I also had a heart condition that required me to take medicine on a daily basis. Only my family and my then doctor knew this. I do not think that my medical condition affected the quality of my work though the rapid sequence of high powered, high stress, jobs in the last ten years of my service left me tired and heightened my sense of anxiety about the future. (In fact my major heart attack was still six years off, but I did not know it at the time.) But none of this appeared in public and, indeed, I understand that Whitehall regarded Robert Armstrong and me as a very laid-back team. They were of course wrong, at any rate as far as I was concerned, because my seemingly unflappable exterior hid a good deal of inner turmoil. I was after all, climbing up my twentieth learning curve. Add to all this what seemed at the time like a bleak outlook for employment after retirement (some of my friends had had a rough time finding work) coupled with a relatively young family still seeking to establish themselves in the world of work, and I began, for the first time, to abandon Oliver Cromwell's comforting doctrine that 'None climbs so high as he who knows not whither he is going.' In short, I got itchy feet.

Events then conspired to offer me a way through my problems. Among other tasks undertaken by the office was responding to outside requests for people, usually retired, to take up jobs outside immediate government service. One interesting one that came to my notice was for a senior person to become director general of the shipping industry's trade association cum industrial relations negotiating body cum defence planning associate of the MoD cum training organization for seamen and cum organizer of a variety of international shipping organizations dealing with bodies like the EEC. But interesting or not this job was not a realistic option for me because, under the terms of my employment, I could only take up such a post three months after leaving the service. And, as I could not afford to lose three months pay, I had to forget it. So my troops went on trying to find a suitable candidate or candidates without much success. Then the gods conspired again. Sultan Quaboos, the ruler of Oman, asked HMG for help in reorganizing his civil service. In consequence, one of my retired chaps had been sent to Oman to have a look at the situation and to produce draft terms of reference for a study. He did so but was unable to go the next mile (as I for one had expected him to do) and undertake the study himself. The study, which was to extend into most aspects of civil service activity in Oman, was expected to take three months to complete and to require a team of five or six experts from the UK plus one of those new-fangled word processor operators. Such a team was therefore assembled. The experts were an outside (but ex-civil service) consultant with experience in manpower planning, a senior man from customs and excise, two experienced personnel managers and trainers from the Cabinet Office (MPO), an Arabic specialist from the FCO, a formidable young lady from the Cabinet Office to play with the gizmo and, eventually, myself as leader with wide experience of how governments actually work.

It will be seen that the three-month time span for the Omani study neatly filled the 'sanitation' gap needed for the shipping job. So, forgetting all about 'Ks' and minor considerations of that kind, I shut my eyes and jumped when the shipping industry knocked on my door and made me an offer better than anything then available in the civil service: more money, a contract to age 65 (with the possibility of further extension by agreement), a large wodge of life insurance, a motorcar for private use, another with chauffeur for office use, and an understanding that if I went abroad on business my wife could come with me expenses paid. The latter point was particularly welcome to both Suzanne and me because the wives of travelling civil servants have to resign themselves to grass widowhood.

Thus, in the autumn of 1983 I signed my letter of resignation from the occupation that had held me in thrall for 34 years and had yielded me an immense amount of interest, pleasure and good companionship. It was not the easiest thing I have ever done in my life.

34

Into the Wild Blue Yonder

On the evening of Friday 28 September 1983 I left my office in Whitehall for the last time. On the evening of Sunday 30 September 1983 I caught a plane at Heathrow bound for Oman to take up the first stage of my new life. This abrupt change provided the antidote to the nostalgia that could so easily have overwhelmed me at that critical moment.

THE END

Index

Admiralty, 49, 217
Agriculture, Ministry of, 13, 19, 45
Air Training Corps, 1
American Declaration of Independence, 174
American Revolution, 88
Anne, Queen, 115
Annie's Bar, 165
Arbed steel works, 74
Ardennes, 73, 81, 159
Armstrong, Robert, 173, 194, 219, 223
Armstrong, Sir William, 129
Army Act, 22
Asquith, Herbert Henry, 88
Atlantic, 19, 81
Atomic and Economic Communities, 65
Attlee, Clement, 18, 86
Attlee, Mrs, 101
Australia, 69

Baldwin, Stanley, 40
Balogh, Tommy, 105–6
Bancroft, Ian, 199
Bank of England, 13
Bannerman, Sir Henry Campbell, 88
Barnett, Correlli, 2

Barnsley, 82–3
Barry, 6
Bastogne, 81
BEA, 78
Beeching, Dr, 46, 190
Belgium, 75
Belgravia, 39, 41
Benelux, 77
Benn, Tony, 121, 151, 155–7, 159–60, 164
Berlaymont, 137
Berrill, Sir Kenneth, 195
Beveridge, 207
Birmingham, 39
Blair, Tony, 142
Boer War, 88, 220
Bolshoi, 103
Bournemouth, 15
BP, 15
Branson, Sir Richard, 222
Bridges, Sir Edward, 4, 173
British Iron and Steel Federation, 65
British Overseas Airways, 42
British Rail, 190
Brook, Norman, 173–4
Brown, George, 105, 110
Brown, Gill, 148
Brussels, 28, 70, 73, 78, 80, 102,

120–1, 130, 134, 136–7, 140, 149, 157, 167, 170, 172, 203
BSE, 19, 163
Bulganin, Nikolay, 44
Burma, 10, 24, 57
Butler, Rab, 12
Butler, Robin, 194, 198
Butler, Victor, 12
Byatt, Ian, 80

Cabinet Office, 4, 15, 17, 33, 37–8, 49, 54, 79, 83, 85–91, 98, 125, 131, 172, 175, 178, 186, 203–4, 214–15, 217, 224
Calcutt, David, 209
Callaghan, Jim, 179, 182
Camberley, 196
Carrington, Peter, 142
Carter, Jimmy, 222
Cassels, John, 215
Catholic Church, 28, 80
Central Electricity Authority, 46
Central Policy Review Staff (CPRS), 144, 195
Channel, 59, 125, 140, 150, 213
Channel Islands, 125
Charles I, 114
Chataway, Chris, 134, 135
Chrysler Motor Company, 64
Churchill, Sir Winston, 18, 40–1, 165
CIA, 160
Citrine, Sir Walter (later Lord), 46
Civil Aviation, Ministry of, 42
Civil Service Arbitration Tribunal, 209
Civil Service Benevolent Society, 7
Civil Service College, 216–17
Civil Service Commission, 122
Civil Service Department (CSD), 199, 203–5, 207, 212, 217

Civil War, 87, 114, 220
cold war, 167
Common Agricultural Policy (CAP), 19, 131, 138
Common Fisheries Policy, 131, 138
Common Market, 73, 103, 120, 123–4, 129, 140
Commonwealth, 65, 69
Confederation of British Industry (CBI), 134
Conference on International Cooperation, 168
Conference on International Economic Cooperation (CIEC), 167
Congress, 111, 147
Conservative government, 129
Conservative Party, 41, 121, 143, 165, 181–2, 212
Corby, 67
Council of Foreign Ministers, 171
Council of Ministers, 156–7
Cripps, Francis, 155
Critchel Down, 117
Croatian, 28
Cromwell, Oliver, 25, 79, 87, 94, 101, 223

Davies, John, 134
Davignon, Steve, 147
Day, Sir Graham, 207
de Gaulle, Charles, 59–60, 62, 80, 133, 139, 172
Deighton, Len, 85
Denehy, Moira, 122
Denman, Sir Roy, 131
Department of Trade and Industry (DTI), 121, 124, 129–31, 135
Dover, 149
Downing Street, 86, 112
Dresden, 25
DSS, 166

Dundee, 135

East India Company, 115
École Nationale d'Administration
  (ENA), 28, 76, 140, 201
École Polytechnique, 28, 140
Eden, John, 135, 182
Egypt, 141
Eighth Army, 124
Energy Council, 156
Energy, Department of, 142, 149
Esher, 123
Euratom, 73, 120
European Coal and Steel
  Community, 20, 65, 73, 120
European Commission, 28, 69, 79,
  120, 134, 136–7, 139, 157,
  167–8, 184
European Court, 171
European Economic Community
  (EEC), 19, 28, 32, 69, 75, 99,
  120, 131–2, 138–9, 143,
  156–7, 167, 170–1, 201, 224
European Union (EU), 19, 27, 29,
  67, 147, 157, 172
Ezra, Derek, 15

Federation of British Industry,
  208
Ferguson, Sir Donald, 5
Fernandel, 7, 54
Fernyhough, Ernie, 105
First Division Association, 7
First World War, 2, 9, 77, 88,
  124
Fleet Air Arm, 55
Ford Motor Company, 181
Foreign and Commonwealth
  Office (FCO), 42, 73, 75, 97,
  103, 132–3, 148, 219, 224
Foreign Office, 102, 132, 158
Forestry Commission, 4
Fourteenth Army, 10, 24, 57

France, 9, 11, 34, 38–9, 51, 60–2,
  67, 75, 99, 101, 104, 115, 132,
  138–9, 142, 158, 161–2, 171,
  203, 214
Franklin, Benjamin, 174
French Revolution, 88, 138, 205
Fuel and Power, Ministry of, 3, 22,
  33, 41, 45, 51
Fulton, Lord, 114; Fulton
  Committee, 114, 207, 218;
  Fulton Report, 67, 116, 200–1

George I, 87
Germany, 28, 35, 75, 99, 138, 139
Gestapo, 11, 53, 138, 168
Giles, Carl, 9
Glasgow, 66
Glorious Revolution, 22, 87, 114
Goodman, Arnold, 105, 106
Gottlieb, Bernard, 120
Grenfell, Joyce, 103
Griffith, Jim, 68
Guernsey, 1, 63
Guiseppe, 59, 148

Hague, The, 159
Hall, Sir Robert, 17
Hampton Court, 91, 118
Hankey, Maurice, 84, 89, 173
Healey, Denis, 83, 184, 210
Heath, Edward, 74, 75, 121, 138,
  144, 194
Heathrow, 149, 226
Helsby, Sir Laurence, 97
Herbecq, John, 199
Heseltine, Michael, 221
Hiroshima, 25
Holloway, 4
Home Civil Service, 114, 116, 199
Home Guard, 1, 68, 220
Home, Alec Douglas, 92
Horny, Suzanne Elisabeth, 63
Horse Guards Parade, 86, 87, 118

Index

Hotel Kléber, 138
Hotel Metropole, 121
House of Commons, 23, 47, 88, 97–8, 102, 106, 109–12, 134–5, 152, 165, 174, 182
House of Lords, 153, 174
Household Cavalry Regiment, 87
Hunt, John, 137, 173, 194
Hurst Park, 118

Iceland, 23
Immingham, 66
India, 103
Indian Army, 57
Indian Civil Service, 6
Indonesia, 57
Industrial Revolution, 88
Industry Act (1972), 129, 133
Ingham, Bernard, 142–3, 146
International Energy Agency, 143, 146
IRA, 165
Iron and Steel Board (ISB), 64, 66
Ironsides, 79, 87
Israel, 141
Italy, 10

James II, 115
James, Henry, 104
Jarratt, Alex, 95
Jarrow, 106
Jenkins, Roy, 184
John, 173
Johnson, Samuel, 29

Kaufman, Gerald, 105–6
KGB, 44, 53, 176
Khrushchev, Nikita, 44
Kingston upon Thames, 63, 72
Koestler, Arthur, 30

Labour Party, 15, 30, 41, 45, 52, 68, 87, 95, 105–6, 111, 117, 141, 143, 151–2, 156, 165, 173, 178–9, 181, 182, 186, 190, 192, 194, 207
Labour, Ministry of, 182
Law, Bonar, 89
Le Cheminant, John, 72
Le Cheminant, Oliver, 72
Le Cheminant, Philip, 80
Le Cheminant, Suzanne, 63, 74, 80, 105, 119, 137, 170, 225
Le Touquet, 149
Lenin, V. I., 127, 167
Liberal Democrats, 182
Liberal Party, 45, 178, 179, 187
Lille, 150
Liverpool, 182
Llanwern, 66
Lloyd George, David, 85, 88, 173
Lloyd, Geoffrey, 39, 40, 44, 46, 48
London, 1, 7, 14, 24, 32, 44, 68, 73, 78–80, 91, 103, 120, 140, 149, 160, 211, 221
London County Council (LCC), 1
London School of Economics (LSE), 1, 10, 49, 54
Lorraine, 74
Lowry, L. S., 9
Luftwaffe, 70
LuxAir, 78
Luxembourg, 65, 73–4, 76–8, 80, 82, 149, 158, 184
Lydd, 149
Lytham St Anne's, 32

Mabon, Dr Dickson, 156
Macaulay Report, 115
MacAuliffe, General, 81
Machiavelli, Niccolò, 201
Macmillan, Harold, 101–2, 164
Malaysia, 18
Malta, 70

Index

Management and Personnel Office
    (MPO), 214–15, 217, 223–4
Mandalay, 24
Maquis, 21
Marston Moor, 79
Mary II, 115
Maude, Sir John, 70
Megaw, Sir John, 199; Megaw
    Inquiry, 201, 207, 208, 210
Melbourne, William Lamb, 177
Messina, 20
Middle East, 141, 156, 168, 169
Midlands, 39, 67
Militant Tendency, 178, 179, 182
Millbank, 21, 44
Mineworkers' Federation of Great
    Britain, 26
Ministry of Defence (MoD), 33,
    142, 217, 223
Ministry of Economics, 31
Ministry of Works, 20
MinTech, 121
Mitchell, Derek, 97
Mole, River, 119
Molotov, Vyacheslav, 133
Montgomery, Sir Bernard, 124
Morgan, Henry, 2, 3
Morrell, Frances, 155, 159
Moscow, 103
Mountbatten, Earl, 98, 104
Munich, 40

Nancy, 161
Napoleon, 115, 171, 220
Naseby, 87
National Economic Development
    Office (NEDDY), 215
National Farmers' Union, 18, 19
National Health Service (NHS),
    191, 213
NATO, 77
Nazi, 31, 139
NCB, 15, 31

Noel, 38
Norfolk, 56
Norman Conquest, 114
Normandy, 10, 21, 39, 102
North Sea, 95, 143, 155
Northamptonshire, 68, 87
Northcote–Trevelyan Report, 115,
    116
Northern Ireland, 128, 151
Northolt, 158
North–South divide, 168
Norway, 146, 149

OAS, 60
OECD, 58, 59, 69, 120, 143, 146
Ofwat, 80
Oman, 224, 226
Oradour-sur-Glane, 138
Organization of Petroleum-
    Exporting Countries, 146, 147
Orly, 59

Palace of Whitehall, 87
Palace Yard, 113
Palliser, Michael, 102
Paris, 58, 73, 78, 137–8, 146, 149,
    160–1, 167, 168
Parliament Act, 88
Parliament Square, 113
Part, Sir Anthony, 124–5, 130
Passchendaele, 101
Persia, Shah of, 142, 159, 160
Piaff, Edith, 205
Pompidou, Georges, 104, 137, 138
Power, Ministry of, 64, 73, 95,
    120, 121, 142
Priestley Commission, 207
Priestley Royal Commission, 197
Proust, Marcel, 57
Public Accounts Committee (PAC),
    111

Quaboos, Sultan, 224

Index

Quai d'Orsay, 133

RAF, 10, 39
Reading, Lady, 53
Reagan, Ronald, 193
Reform Acts, 88
Regent Street Polytechnic, 15
Regional Development Fund, 138, 140
Reid, Malcolm, 104
Representatives, House of, 147
Restoration, 114
Reykjavik, 23, 78
Rhine, 163
Richard, Thomas & Baldwin, 66, 71
Richmond, 60
Richmond Park, 63
Richmond Terrace, 86
Richmond-upon-Thames, 72
Rolls-Royce, 128
Rome, 20
Rothschild, Victor, 144
Royal Engineers, 24
Ruhr, 31
Rupert, Prince, 87
Russia, 31, 56, 162, 174

Sabena, 78
Salerno, 59, 148
Salvation Army, 53
Scilly Isles, 106, 107
Scotland, 66, 125, 128, 151
Searle, Ronald, 181
Second World War, 2, 10, 24, 25, 138, 171, 173
Shastri, Lal, 103
Sheen, 63
Sinn Fein, 165
Smiles, Samuel, 169
Smith, Adam, 147
Smith, John, 156
SNCF, 150

Soames, Christopher, 205
South Africa, 72
South Wales, 66
Soviet, 44, 51, 141, 176, 177
Soviet Union, 44, 51, 188
Spaak, Marie, 103
Spaak, Paul-Henri, 103
Sports and Social Council, 34
SS, 21, 31, 38, 138
St Mary's, 107
Steel Company of Wales, 66
Stevenson, Robert Louis, 165
Stoke D'Abernon Manor, 3
Strasbourg, 60, 76
Stromboli, 60
Suez Canal, 51
Suez crisis, 51, 52, 55
Supply, Ministry of, 64–5, 69
Sweden, 12, 47
Switzerland, 154
Sydney, 69
Syria, 141

Taffy, 39
Tebbit, Norman, 184
Technology, Ministry of, 121
Tehran, 159
Thames, 91, 221
Thatcher, Margaret, 46, 123, 173, 181–2, 184, 186–8, 192, 195–7, 221
Thomas, George, 110
Torrey Canyon, 107
Treasury, 4, 13, 17, 30, 32–3, 42, 46, 49, 57, 80, 82, 86, 95, 97, 115, 120, 128–9, 132, 136, 190, 194, 200, 203–7, 212, 218, 220
Trend, Sir Burke, 95, 173
Truman, Harry S., 97, 193
TUC, 46
Twickenham, 72

UK, 19, 27, 47, 56, 66, 72, 73, 79,

87, 120, 132, 134, 146, 147, 151, 155–6, 170, 190, 191, 193, 224
UN, 168, 169, 172
United Front, 139
United Nations Association, 112
United States, 7, 12, 23, 35, 41–2, 51, 56, 101, 107, 111, 146–7, 153–4, 158, 172, 193, 200, 208, 222
Upper-Clyde Shipbuilders, 128

Varley, Eric, 105, 143, 151
Victoria, 15, 125, 217
Victoria station, 149
Victoria Street, 134
Vietnam, 110

Wales, 39, 41, 66, 68, 110, 125, 128, 151
Walpole, Robert, 87, 203
Walters, Peter, 15
War of Independence, 220
War Office, 2
Washington, 12, 60
Watford, 162
Watkinson, Sir Lawrence, 34, 35, 36
Webb, Sidney and Beatrix, 188
Wehrmacht, 39

West Indies, 98
West Lothian, 152
Westminster, 20, 152, 153, 165, 174
Westminster, Palace of, 112
White House, 97
Whitehall, 3, 17, 19–21, 26, 33, 37, 43, 49, 51, 57, 64, 68, 85–7, 92, 99, 101, 111, 115, 122, 125, 132, 165–6, 173–4, 176, 186, 194–5, 199, 204, 206, 211, 216–17, 223, 226
Whitelaw, William, 194
Wigg, George, 23, 105, 106, 110, 111
William III, 115
Williams, Leonard, 170, 184
Williams, Marcia, 100
Wilson, Harold, 92, 97, 100, 104–5, 111, 113, 143–4, 155
Wilson, Jimmy, 70
Woodfield, Philip, 98
Workers Education Association (WEA), 15
Wright, Oliver, 97, 102
WVS (now WRVS), 53, 54

Yom Kippur War, 120, 131, 141
York University, 5